THE 50 GREATEST ARCHITECTS

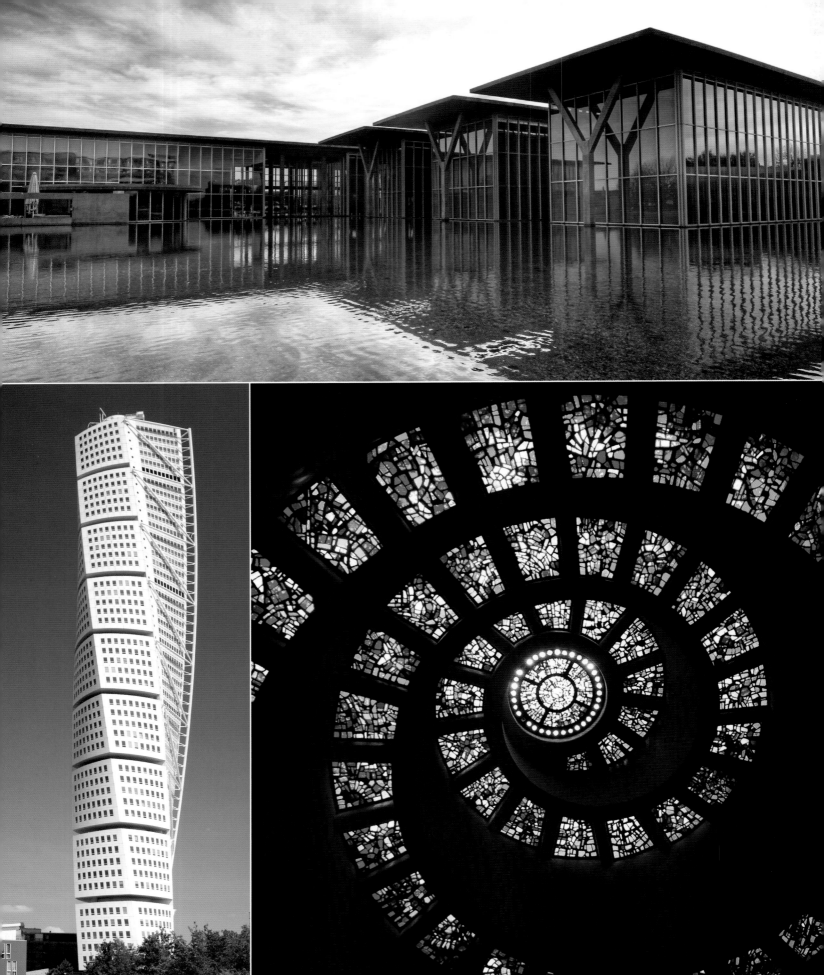

THE 50 GREATEST ARCHITECTS

THE PEOPLE WHOSE BUILDINGS HAVE SHAPED OUR WORLD

IKE IJEH

ARCTURUS

ARCTURUS

This edition published in 2021 by Arcturus Publishing Limited
26/27 Bickels Yard, 151–153 Bermondsey Street,
London SE1 3HA

ISBN: 978-1-83857-420-8
AD008038UK

Printed in China

CONTENTS

INTRODUCTION

Greatness is by its very nature reductive and subjective. By conferring greatness on some, one implicitly confers inferiority on others – it is clearly a naïve and simplistic means of assessment. Equally, criticism of any kind is almost always subjective, as opinion marks the death of objectivity.

And yet there is an innate codifying trait in human nature that yearns for hierarchy and elevation. Even the most primitive human existences arranged their societies into variations of what we might today call the class system, and this primeval preoccupation with conferring seniority upon a select few informs our cultural, political, social and civic fabric to this day.

Nowhere are these habits more ingrained than in the arts, which, unlike science, are all about subjectivity. We have great composers, great artists, great writers and of course great architects. As an art form, architecture is unique: it is the only one with which we have no choice but to engage. A blind person may not be able to view the glories of a Baroque fresco, but they must navigate walls and maybe stairs to reach their bedroom every night. So those architects we deem as great have far more potential to affect our everyday lives than the Mozarts, Tolstoys and Canalettos we may (gratefully) encounter in other exhalted disciplines.

LEFT: UNESCO decribed Sydey Opera House (Jørn Utzon; p.140) as 'a great architectural work of the 20th century'.

ABOVE: St. Peter's Square (Gian Lorenzo Bernini; p.40) is one of the most famous public spaces in the world and is adjacent to the world's largest church.

This book therefore attempts to identify fifty architects who might be considered the greatest of their profession. Your author has no illusions about the subjectivity of the choices or the borderline futility of the exercise. Compressing 5,000 years of human civilization – with all the styles, periods, epochs and movements that generated – into one digestible tome was always bound to be an exercise of omission more than inclusion.

Equally, some may smart at obvious omissions. Despite their substantial contributions to the world of architecture, there was no room for Jules Hardouin-Mansart, Claude-Nicolas Ledoux, Robert Adam, Augustus Welby Pugin, Alvar Aalto, Luis Barragán and Shigeru Ban. Not because they do not make the greatness grade, but simply because of the need for expediency over exhaustiveness imposed by the literary format.

But despite the subjectivity and discrimination, there is still a profound value to the selection that unfolds on the following pages, for each architect tells us something about their environment, culture, constraints and principles and about how architecture has helped form the world in which we live.

Also, in each architect's catalogue of human triumphs and disappointments, we can find tools to conquer adversity and inspire us too to greater things. Of all art forms, architecture is ultimately a human story, and the most rewarding aspect of unravelling that story and shedding light on those who have made it great is that we learn a little something about ourselves.

HEMIUNU

ONLY ONE OF THE SEVEN WONDERS OF THE ANCIENT WORLD STILL EXISTS, AND IT IS THE OLDEST OF THEM ALL.

EGYPT b. 2570 BCE

HIGHLIGHTS:
The Great Pyramid of Giza

PRINCIPAL STYLE:
Fourth Dynasty of Ancient Egypt

ABOVE: Hemiunu

The Great Pyramid of Giza is the largest and most famous of Egypt's approximately 130 ancient pyramids, and it has helped make the pyramid one of the most recognizable architectural objects in the world, featuring even on the American dollar bill.

Despite the huge role the Ancient Egyptian pyramids have played in our culture, civilization and iconography, their creators are shrouded in secrecy. But the architect behind Giza's Great Pyramid led a life of power and prestige that almost mirrored that of the great pharaohs whom the pyramids were built to entomb.

Hemiunu was born into the Egyptian royal family. His parents were a prince and princess, and his uncle was Khufu, second pharaoh of the Fourth Dynasty, who commissioned the building of the Great Pyramid and, Egyptologists believe, was entombed in it when he died. But the familial relation who arguably had the biggest impact on Hemiunu's life and career was his grandfather Pharaoh Sneferu.

Since the beginning of the ancient dynastic period in Egypt, around 3100 BCE, kings and rulers had been buried in mastabas: squat, trapezoidal, flat-roofed structures crudely constructed from mud bricks. It was the great architect Imhotep, later deified as a healing god, who first thought of stacking smaller and smaller mastabas on top of each other, and thus the pyramid tomb was born. Early pyramids were stepped in profile; it wasn't until Sneferu's rule that the smooth outline we recognize today was introduced. Sneferu also established innovations to pyramids' internal structure.

Hemiunu would have been well aware of these changes when he succeeded his father as vizier, the

RIGHT: Hemiunu's most powerful legacy, The Great Pyramid at Giza.

most senior position in the royal court – roughly equivalent to prime minister today. Crucially, he was also the royal architect, which meant he oversaw all royal construction projects. In this capacity Hemiunu built the Great Pyramid at Giza. Comprising almost 2.8 million cubic metres (100 million cubic feet) and weighing an estimated 5.5 million tonnes (almost 945 million stone), the structure took around two decades to construct and was built on a scale never previously seen in Egypt. Originally almost 147 m (482 ft) high,

for almost 4,000 years it was the tallest building in the world, only surpassed by Lincoln Cathedral in the 14th century.

All pyramids conformed to largely the same geometric and decorative precepts, and Hemiunu had little opportunity to place his architectural stamp on his creation. But he managed it in three ways. The most obvious is Giza's gigantic scale. This has political as well as architectural significance. Like Europe's baroque palaces, the scale of pyramids

was directly proportional to the level of absolutism practised by their sovereigns; when authoritarianism and centralization declined under future dynasties, pyramids became smaller and pharaohs built more logistically feasible temples instead.

Hemiunu's second stamp is the gleaming white limestone blocks in which the pyramid was originally encased. These were later eroded or deliberately dismantled. Symbolically, the form of the ancient pyramids was said to be derived from the descending rays of the sun, and in order to convey the impression of glistening luminescence, most pyramids were clad with this limestone skin. Giza's surface aimed to be the most polished and reflective of them all and was

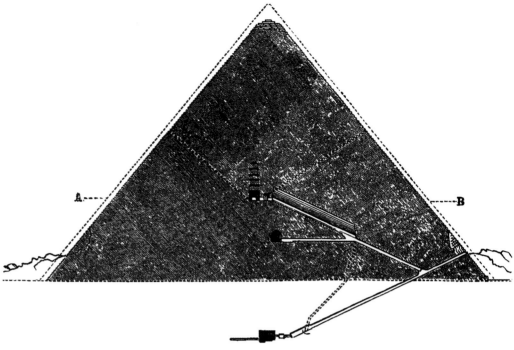

ABOVE: A drawing of a cross section of the Great Pyramid of Giza.

LEFT: An example of a mastaba, the tomb style that predated pyramids in Ancient Egypt.

BELOW RIGHT: *Stella octangula*, an engraving by Leonardo da Vinci showing the golden ratio as used in the form of the Great Pyramid, from *De Divina Proportione* by Luca Pacioli, published 1509, Venice.

are said to derive. Long after the demise of Ancient Egypt, the ratio fascinated the Ancient Greeks; even in the Renaissance, Leonardo da Vinci based the composition of his *Mona Lisa* on its strictures. If Hemiunu did the same, then he was perhaps the first architect to formalize humankind's enduring pursuit of beauty, order and perfection through architecture, an obsession that would become a defining feature of civilization for centuries to come.

said to shine like a star in the desert – so much so that Ancient Egyptians referred to it as *Ikhet*, which means 'Glorious Light'.

Hemiunu's most powerful legacy comes in Giza's proportions. The Great Pyramid's dimensions closely match the golden ratio, a mathematical principle from which beauty and perfection in art and nature

MARCUS
VITRUVIUS POLLIO

ITALY 80–70 BCE – 15 CE

HIGHLIGHTS
Basilica di Fano

PRINCIPAL STYLE
Roman Classicism

ABOVE: Vitruvius

VERY FEW BOOKS HAVE TRANSFORMED THE WORLD. THE BIBLE – PARTICULARLY THE KING JAMES VERSION – IS ONE. *ON THE ORIGIN OF SPECIES, THE COMMUNIST MANIFESTO* AND *A DICTIONARY OF THE ENGLISH LANGUAGE* ARE OTHERS.

Also on this list is a lesser-known title, a seminal polemical treatise completed fifteen years before Christ and dedicated to Emperor Caesar Augustus. It would establish the founding principles to which architecture has adhered ever since.

De Architectura libri decem, now more commonly known as *Ten Books on Architecture*, is the most influential book on architecture ever written. Its author was a Roman architect and military engineer who sought to codify for the first time the rules and principles on which architecture should be based. Marcus Vitruvius Pollio served in the Roman army as an engineer, initially designing combat artillery. The contrast would not have seemed strange then: architecture in the Roman Empire was a broad term that included a variety of technical disciplines, including construction management, urban planning, civil engineering and mechanical design.

But it was buildings to which Vitruvius chiefly turned his attention, and in *De Architectura* he provides a guide for how buildings should be designed. Books 1 to VI deal directly with architecture and town planning, and the remaining four books explore more

BELOW: The Pantheon in Rome was inspired by the principles of architecture first laid down by Vitruvius.

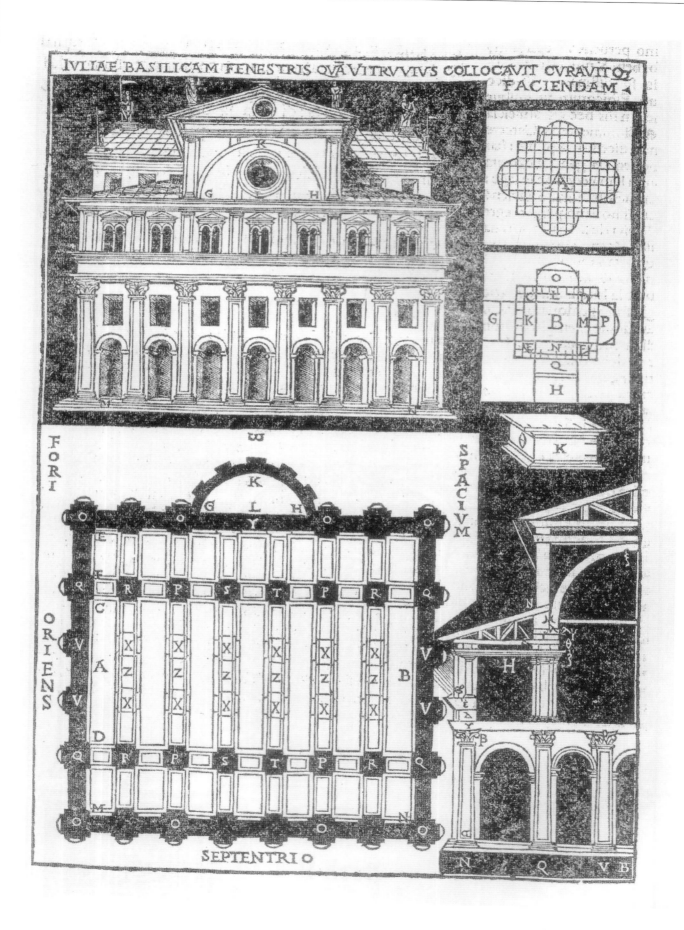

prosaic disciplines such as irrigation, machinery and plasterwork. Throughout, Vitruvius attempts to define how architecture can achieve aesthetic beauty through an understanding of elements such as order, arrangement, symmetry, balance and proportion, and he does so with an almost scientific sense of theoretical precision.

In the most famous passage, in Book 1, Vitruvius states that all buildings should have three core characteristics: strength, utility and beauty (updated by later scholars to firmness, commodity and delight). Two millennia later, this extract is familiar to architecture students across the world and indicates the clarity and pragmatism with which Vitruvius distilled complex ideas for a wide audience.

It is impossible to overstate *De Architectura*'s influence on architecture, Western civilization and global culture. After Vitruvius's death, scores of iconic Roman buildings, such as the Pantheon, the Roman Forum and the Baths of Diocletian, were designed according to his book's principles. His work influenced great figures of Renaissance and classical architecture, including Filippo Brunelleschi (p.20), Andrea Palladio (p.32) and Inigo Jones (p.36).

Leonardo da Vinci was captivated by him. In his *Vitruvian Man* of 1490, da Vinci mathematically applied Vitruvian principles of symmetry and proportion to the greatest work of art of all, the human body.

These principles also inspired the neoclassical stylistic movements of the 15th to 19th centuries and helped drive the postmodern and new classical ideologies of the late 20th and early 21st centuries. One of the most famous books of British architecture, Colen Campbell's *Vitruvius Britannicus* (1715–25), was directly inspired by its Roman forebear and sought to purge what it saw as the emotional excesses of Baroque with Vitruvian-inspired ideals of Palladian purity. A Danish version was published soon after, and both were intellectually anchored to the Age of Enlightenment, itself Vitruvian in its search for rationality and order.

Vitruvian ideals came to be principally associated with classical architecture, but in *De Architectura*'s forensic focus on spatial and aesthetic generalities, such as light and movement, Vitruvius established an idealized framework that could be applied to any number of styles. The book was also a groundbreaking work of engineering, with early designs for hoists, cranes, building services, acoustics, pipework, aqueducts, steam engines, surveying tools and even central heating, many of which informed the development of our modern equivalents.

Vitruvius may not have designed many buildings, and next to nothing is known about his sole major architectural commission, a long-vanished basilica in Fano, Italy. Nor did he necessarily invent all the ideas in *De Architectura*: in its reliance on established theories relating to themes like classical orders and mechanical engineering, he is more classifier than creator. But there can be no doubt that in attempting to intellectually codify architecture for the first time, Vitruvius established many of the aesthetic principles on which two millennia of human civilization would be built.

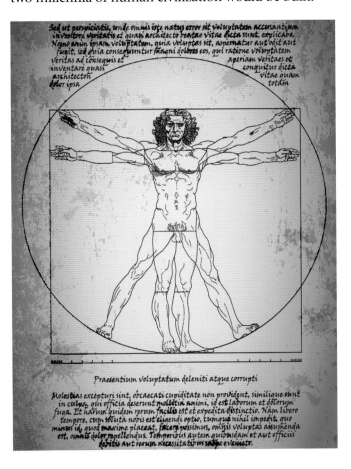

LEFT: The plans by Vitruvius for the Basilica di Fano.

RIGHT: Leonardo da Vinci was inspired by the work of Vitruvius to apply his principles of symmetry to the human body.

HENRY YEVELE

ENGLAND 1320–1400

HIGHLIGHTS
Westminster Abbey, Canterbury Cathedral

PRINCIPAL STYLE
Gothic

ABOVE: A boss believed to depict Henry Yevele

HENRY YEVELE WAS NOT ONLY THE MOST PROLIFIC AND SUCCESSFUL MASTER MASON OF THE ENGLISH MIDDLE AGES, HE ALSO HELPED ESTABLISH THE IDEA OF GOTHIC ARCHITECTURE AS A UNIQUE EXPRESSION OF ENGLISH CULTURAL CONSCIOUSNESS AND NATIONAL IDENTITY, IDEAS THAT WOULD RESONATE POWERFULLY DURING THE 19TH-CENTURY GOTHIC REVIVAL.

The Gothic style originated in France in the early 12th century, developing from Romanesque as an artistic movement designed to project the dynastic ambitions of the French monarchy. It was associated mostly with religious architecture and flourished across Europe.

Where Romanesque featured round arches, small windows, thick walls and sober decoration, Gothic found its signature motif in the pointed arch and embraced larger windows, lighter walls and ostentatious ornamentation. Two elements especially defined the style: God and structure. The pointed arch

RIGHT: The nave of Westminster Abbey.

LEFT: The Jewel Tower, one of only two surviving sections of the medieval Palace of Westminster, believed to have been designed by Henry Yevele.

was a symbolic arrow pointing towards the heavens, and Gothic churches and cathedrals rapturously embraced height to elevate humankind towards the celestial firmament. To achieve this, Gothic became an exercise in extreme structural dexterity, with elaborate vaulting to support lofty ceilings, and flying buttresses to stabilize thinner walls punctuated by gigantic stained-glass windows.

By the time Yevele, a successful Derbyshire mason, was appointed by the Black Prince to reconstruct his great hall at Kennington Manor in 1357, he would have been intimately familiar with the Gothic movement,

which was firmly established in England. But it was not until the Prince's father, Edward III, appointed Yevele his deviser (designer) of masonry – essentially responsible for all Crown works – three years later that his career took flight.

Yevele remodelled works to various royal properties, including the Tower of London, Westminster Hall and the Palace of Westminster; supervised repairs and additions to Durham Cathedral, Southampton Carisbrooke and Winchester Castles; and designed tombs for royalty and aristocracy.

During his long career there were two areas where he would have long-lasting influence. The first was in establishing what became the Office of the King's Works in 1378, which he ran in its capacity as successor to the deviser of masonry role. This institution would produce some of the greatest works of English royal and public architecture for the next 400 years.

The second was in his pioneering supervision of a large workshop responsible not just for the construction of buildings but also for their conceptualization and design. Yevele redefined the role of a traditional medieval master mason. In turning the architect from an artisan to an artist, he helped bridge the gap between the Middle Ages and the Renaissance.

For Yevele's cultural legacy, we return to the style he made his own. His architectural career is still defined by his work on the two pre-eminent buildings in the global Anglican Communion and two of the most important Gothic structures in medieval Christendom: Westminster Abbey (1376–87) and Canterbury Cathedral (1377–1400). At Westminster he completed the nave that was unfinished since the death of Henry III, and at Canterbury he rebuilt the old Romanesque nave that for decades had been in ruins.

English cathedrals were known for their great length (Winchester remains the longest Gothic cathedral in

Europe), French ones for their tremendous height. At Westminster, Yevele combined both traditions, crafting the highest nave in England at 31 m (102 ft) and creating a highly ornamental interior with spectacular gold-ribbed lierne vaulting and gleaming Purbeck marble piers that forms a paragon of the Decorated English Gothic style.

He took things further at Canterbury, where the astonishing uniformity and decorative consistency of his magnificent nave, along with the use of flattened arches and extreme geometric intricacy, forms an early example of large-scale Perpendicular architecture, the final phase of the Gothic period in England.

Both are archetypes of English Gothic architecture and have helped cement Gothic into the British consciousness. They had a profound effect on 19th-century culture, when the Victorians revived Gothic architecture as a style whose fantastical physical form spoke to a highly idealized and romanticized view of medieval antiquity, and whose engineering prowess and spiritual purity formed fitting historic precedents for a proud new national identity. Despite Gothic's French origins, from nursery rhymes to Hollywood it has driven a popular perception of medieval England as a halcyon land of castles, cathedrals, chivalry and crennelation – a narrative that Yevele helped write.

FILIPPO
BRUNELLESCHI

ITALY 1377–1446

HIGHLIGHTS
Santa Maria del Fiore, San
Lorenzo Basilica, Santo Spirito
Basilica

PRINCIPAL STYLE
Italian Renaissance

ABOVE: Filippo Brunelleschi

RARELY IN ARCHITECTURE DOES ONE PERSON START A MOVEMENT. WALTER GROPIUS FOUNDED THE BAUHAUS SCHOOL. ANDREA PALLADIO POSTHUMOUSLY INSPIRED PALLADIANISM. INIGO JONES BROUGHT CLASSICISM TO ENGLAND. BUT NONE HAD THE IMPACT OF THE MAN WHO IS ARGUABLY THE PRE-EMINENT FOUNDING FATHER OF RENAISSANCE ARCHITECTURE, THE FLORENTINE GENIUS FILIPPO BRUNELLESCHI.

ABOVE: Interior of the Basilica of San Lorenzo, Florence, Italy.

Not only was Brunelleschi pivotal in establishing the artistic and architectural movement that would usher in the Reformation, the Age of Enlightenment and the modern world, but he was also an artist, engineer, sculptor, clockmaker, goldsmith, mathematician and ship designer. Ancient Greece may have been the birthplace of Western civilization, but Brunelleschi and his successors ensured that by the 14th century, Italy had become its cradle.

Born to a wealthy Florentine family, Brunelleschi received an education in mathematics and was drawn to art, initially as a sculptor. Although he did not design buildings while he carved commissions for Florentine churches, the period gave him a foretaste of the Renaissance doctrines he would soon make his own. It introduced him to the Medici family, who became his lifelong patrons, and to Lorenzo Ghiberti, who became his chief architectural rival.

Medieval culture had been dominated by Byzantine art and Gothic architecture. Both tended to depict figures and decoration in a formal, iconoclastic way.

ABOVE: The famous Santa Maria del Fiore whose dome dominates the Florence skyline.

But a late-14th-century resurgence of interest in the more realistic depictions of Ancient Greece and Rome, and the classical architecture with which they were synonymous, sowed revisionist seeds that would lead to the Renaissance.

Brunelleschi's artistic efforts in response to these developments revolutionized European painting. His experiments led him to conclude that artistic realism was based on the principle of objects receding into infinity. By introducing perspective into Western art, he transformed how civilization depicted the world. Similarly, the more expressive and decorative sculpture with which Brunelleschi was working gave him a grounding in themes he would adopt in his architecture – bolstered by a formative visit to Rome, then largely in ruins.

The first building on which Brunelleschi's stylistic strategies were deployed architecturally was Florence's Foundling Hospital of 1419–45. With its round arches, arcaded loggia, simple decoration, pedimented

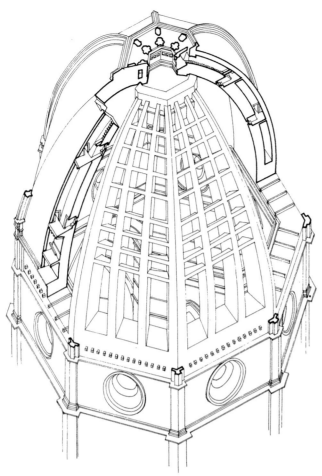

widest dome ever seen. But the Gothic style was so strictly rejected that the flying buttresses which might have supported the structure had been banned by the city authorities.

Brunelleschi's solution was ingenious. He built two brick domes: a thicker inner dome up to 0.6 metres (two feet) wide and a thinner outer dome clad in terracotta tiles that acted as a shell. This enabled a staircase to be inserted between them to reach the lantern at the top; it also ensured more even

windows and Corinthian columns, it rejected medieval Gothic and conspicuously harked back to classical antiquity. As the first building in Florence to do so since the fall of Rome, it caused a sensation. Now widely accepted as the first Renaissance building in Europe, the hospital set a stylistic precedent that defined Brunelleschi's future career and became the model for Renaissance architecture across the continent for 200 years.

Scores of commissions followed, mostly for churches. But Brunelleschi's most famous work, which became an international template for Renaissance architecture, was his dome for Florence Cathedral. Santa Maria del Fiore was begun in 1296, and in 1418, when Brunelleschi was appointed over rival Ghiberti, the building was complete apart from its dome.

The problem was that the intended dome – designed by the city's former master mason Neri di Fioravanti – was thought impossible. With an outer diameter of 54 m (177 ft) and a base 52 m (170 ft) above the floor, Neri's design called for the tallest and distribution of the dome's immense weight. Stability was enhanced by the dome's octagonal shape and by chains at its base to prevent spreading. Finally, by laying the bricks in an innovative herringbone pattern, each layer supported the one above, negating the need for scaffolding. Brunelleschi also devised a pulley to lift the bricks from the ground, anticipating modern cranes and lifts 500 years later.

With four million bricks and weighing 40,000 tonnes (6.3 million stone), the dome of Florence Cathedral remains the largest brick dome in the world. Its revolutionary twin-dome and chain-ring construction influenced domes from Les Invalides in Paris to the US Capitol in Washington DC. An apocryphal story says Brunelleschi won the commission by dropping an egg on a table to prove that the top shell could stand even if the bottom half was smashed. It is comforting to know that the man who changed the course of Western art and architecture had a sense of humour.

KUAI

XIANG

CHINA 1398-1491

HIGHLIGHTS
The Forbidden City

PRINCIPAL STYLE
Ming Dynasty

ABOVE: The Yongle Emperor,
Zhu Di

WHILE 15TH-CENTURY EUROPE WAS EXPERIENCING A CULTURAL REAWAKENING WITH THE RENAISSANCE, CHINA TOO WAS UNDERGOING A PERIOD OF PROGRESS, EXPANSION AND ADVANCEMENT.

The defeat of the Mongols in 1368 had ushered in the more culturally enlightened Ming Dynasty, desperate to reverse the neglect, decline and depopulation wrought by the Mongol invasions.

As part of this national renewal, the Yongle Emperor Zhu Di (pictured left since there are no confirmed portraits of Kuai Xiang), the third Ming ruler, undertook a number of large strategic construction projects. The largest docks in the world were built at Nanjing, then China's capital city and described by some sources as the world's largest city at the time. From Nanjing, vast maritime expeditions set sail across the world, not to conquer and colonize like their European counterparts but to spread Chinese power, influence and prestige.

In the time-honoured autocratic tradition, the emperor wanted more. In 1417 he settled on plans to relocate the capital city to Beijing after rebuilding it with unprecedented imperial splendour. The city plan was regularized into gridded blocks, the city was encircled by a new 15 kilometre (9.3 miles) wall and its Grand Canal network was deepened and enlarged to help ships bring grain to the city's growing population.

The centrepiece of Zhu Di's plans was the construction of a vast new imperial palace in the centre of the Forbidden City. Covering almost 200

BELOW: The entrance to the Forbidden City in Beijing

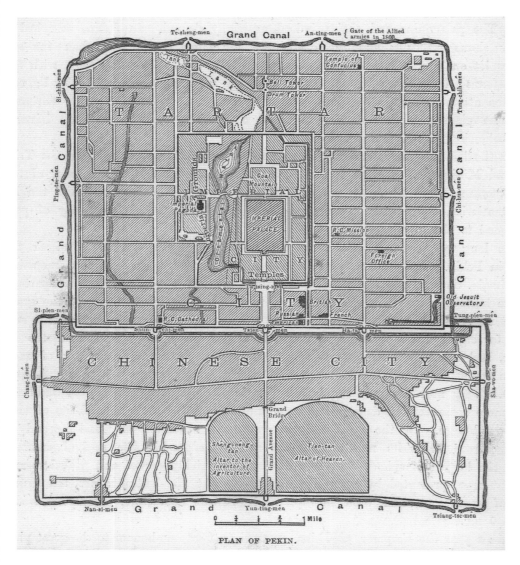

PLAN OF PEKIN.

acres, bigger than Buckingham Palace and Versailles combined, it remains the largest palace complex in the world and endures as a powerful global symbol of Chinese culture and identity. The architect chosen for what may be the most prestigious project in Chinese history was a young engineer called Kuai Xiang.

Xiang was born in Xukou in the eastern Chinese province of Jiansu. Little is known about his youth, but he grew up in Xiangshan, a district famed for its carpentry and crafts. His skills were said to be such that by his early thirties he was the head of the Xiangshan Carpenters, a local association of artisans that still exists today in a heavily altered guise. In this capacity Xiang came to the attention of the emperor, who commanded him to travel north to build the emperor's new palace in Beijing.

ABOVE: Plan of Beijing (Pekin) showing how the Forbidden City is sited within its surrounds.

RIGHT: Tower of the Summer Palace.

26

It was a mammoth undertaking. Construction lasted fourteen years and involved over 100,000 artisans and up to a million workers. But the result is an iconic emblem of Chinese traditional architecture and would serve as the engine room of Chinese imperial rule for 500 years. Xiang arranged monumental halls and temples around an inner and outer court. The outer court contained the grander public buildings, while the inner court led to more private royal domestic accommodation.

The showpiece temples sport gigantic sloping roofs encrusted with golden tiles and supported by elaborately carved wooden brackets set upon marble plinths. Surrounded by their vast sequence of open courtyards, they are all astronomically aligned in perfect symmetry. While Xiang blended traditional Chinese precedents and complied with strict Taoist principles, the authoritative scale and composition of the city was entirely of his own making and has become the standard cultural reference point by which historic Chinese architecture is perceived by the wider world.

BELOW: Detail of doorway within the Forbidden City.

MIMAR SINAN

TURKEY 1489–1588

HIGHLIGHTS
Süleymaniye Mosque, Selimiye Mosque, Şehzade Mosque

PRINCIPAL STYLE
Classical Ottoman

ABOVE: Mimar Sinan

FRANK LLOYD WRIGHT WAS NOT KNOWN FOR HIS MODESTY. SO WHEN HE SAID THERE WERE ONLY TWO ARCHITECTS IN HISTORY WORTH KNOWING ABOUT, HIMSELF AND MIMAR SINAN, ONE'S INTEREST IS NATURALLY PIQUED.

Sinan's is not a name familiar to Western audiences, but he is one of the most influential architects of all time. Designing almost 400 religious and secular buildings in Turkey, Eastern Europe and the Middle East at the peak of the Ottoman Empire, he reshaped the skyline of Constantinople (now Istanbul) into the orgy of domes and minarets we recognize today.

As the greatest architect of the Ottoman classical period and a contemporary of Michelangelo, Sinan was crucial in promoting an architecture that synthesized the Christian and Islamic worlds. He designed spectacular mosques influenced by both cultures, and updated the Byzantine style to a simpler spatial interplay between light and shade that would profoundly influence Le Corbusier centuries later. Such was Sinan's influence that he trained scores of apprentices who had significant architectural impact across the Ottoman Empire and beyond. One of them, Ustad Ahmad Lahori, built the Taj Mahal.

Sinan was born to a stonemason in Agirnas in central Turkey. In a sign of the cross-cultural pollination that would characterize his legacy, he has been variously described as having Armenian, Albanian, Greek and

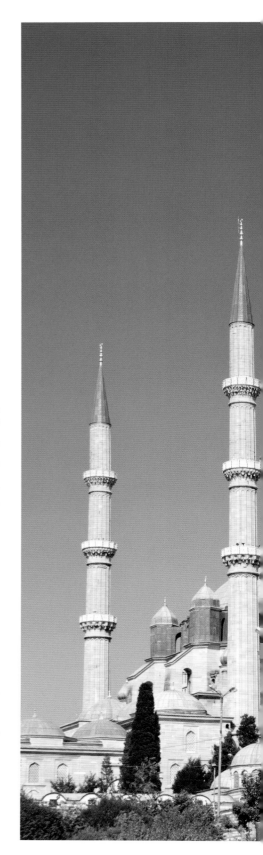

Turkish origins. What is certain is that Sinan was born a Christian and converted to Islam when conscripted into the Ottoman army in his twenties. There he extended the carpentry and stonemasonry skills he had learned under his father, embellishing them with formal engineering and architectural training.

Sinan's architectural career did not get fully under way until he was around fifty, when Grand Vizier Pasha, under whose command he had served, appointed him chief architect for the construction and supervision of all major infrastructural and imperial projects in Istanbul. In this capacity he designed roads, aqueducts, bridges, smaller mosques, schools, mansions, baths, hospitals and government buildings.

Only when he received his first major commission – for a grand mosque to commemorate the death of one of Sultan Suleiman the Magnificent's sons – did his pioneering brilliance come to the fore.

Şehzade Mosque (1548) is the first of three grand Istanbul mosques that Sinan designed that would define his career and legacy. It was built on established themes in Ottoman mosque architecture, such as the use of domes, semi-domes, minarets and courtyards all stylistically and functionally aligned to Byzantine precedents. Much of this tone was set by the Hagia Sophia mosque of ad 537, the largest building in the

BELOW: Süleymaniye Mosque in Istanbul.

ABOVE: Interior of domes within Şehzade Mosque.

world when complete and still the overriding religious and cultural symbol of the city.

But Sinan introduced variations that came to define his work. Şehzade's interior is a single, immense open space with no galleries, allowing for a more dramatic interior with the interplay of light and shade that would so impress Le Corbusier on full display. To support the dome while admitting as much light as possible, buttresses are concealed behind walls which are then externally screened by continuous colonnades.

Seven years later came Sinan's most famous work. Süleymaniye Mosque (1557) in Istanbul incorporates themes deployed at Şehzade, conceived on a much bigger scale and without the use of dome-supporting piers, ensuring a more unified internal space. The courtyard is extraordinary, with an exquisite colonnaded peristyle sumptuously clad in marble and granite and set in perfect symmetry within the mosque's wider geometric composition.

But it is Selimiye Mosque (1574) in Erdine that is considered Sinan's greatest achievement. With four 83 m (272 ft) high minarets, still the tallest in the Muslim world, it is a masterpiece of Islamic architecture. Here the themes of internal unity, spatial organization, geometric precision, spherical interplay and structural harmony came to spectacular fruition. The profusion of domes and half-domes of Sinan's earlier work is superseded by a single gigantic dome and indicates the unifying internal structure that Sinan had achieved.

It is impossible not to see commonalities between Sinan's Islamic domes and the contemporaneous Christian basilicas of Renaissance Europe. The structural challenges he faced with buttresses, piers, arches and geometry were the same facing Michelangelo, Bramante and Wren. In his military youth, Sinan travelled Europe and would have seen much of the Renaissance's output. Michelangelo and Leonardo da Vinci would have been equally aware of the Byzantine origins of Renaissance classical architecture. While Sinan's work rightly stands as a pinnacle of Islamic architecture, the reciprocal cultural relationship it maintained with Western architecture should not be forgotten.

ANDREA
PALLADIO

ITALY 1508–1580

HIGHLIGHTS
Church of San Giorgio
Maggiore, Basilica Palladiana,
Palazzo del Capitaniato
(Vincenza)

PRINCIPAL STYLE
Neoclassical Renaissance

ABOVE: Andrea Palladio

GLOBALIZATION IS OFTEN CONSIDERED A RECENT PHENOMENON, BUT IT IS NOT. TO FIND THE ARCHITECTURAL ORIGINS OF 18TH-CENTURY LONDON, WE MUST TRAVEL TO 16TH-CENTURY VENETO IN NORTH-EASTERN ITALY, SPECIFICALLY THE ELEGANT CITY OF VICENZA.

ABOVE: San Giorgio Maggiore
viewed from Venice shores.

Why? Because the Palladian movement dominated the first half of 18th-century England as it did nowhere else, instigated by the great Renaissance architect Andrea Palladio.

It is impossible to overstate Palladio's impact on Western architecture. His ideas found an audience not just in England but in France, Germany, Ireland, the US, and extensively in his native Italy. That it took centuries for many of these ideas to percolate to their hosts testifies to their endurance. That his movement was named directly after him – a rare honour in architecture – shows how intensely his ideas were interwoven with his person.

The first and most striking way that Palladio announced his intellectual allegiances was by changing his name. Born Andrea di Pietro della Gondola in Padua, he developed an early interest in stonecutting. Moving to nearby Vicenza, he indulged in his other interest, Ancient Rome, under apprenticeships in stonemasonry and architecture. His first architectural commission came at the age of

thirty when he was asked to rebuild the villa of local scholar Gian Giorgio Trissino, another committed student of antiquity. So impressed was Trissino with della Gondola's work that he gave him the name by which he would be known in perpetuity, a reference to Pallas Athene, Greek goddess of wisdom. The cult of Palladianism was born.

That cult looked to antiquity, Ancient Rome in particular, as a moral, cultural and architectural ideal. Palladio based his architecture on strict classical rules

and was heavily influenced by Vitruvius. He too saw classicism as a means to bring order and rationality to an unpredictable world. His buildings prioritized symmetry, perspective, proportion and balance in an effort to attain the beauty and perfection that preoccupied the classical world.

This could not be further from the emotional ostentation of the Baroque age that followed Palladio's death. Long before the boisterous brotherhood of Borromini and Bernini sought melodrama and chaos

at every turn, Palladio strove for propriety and order, the balm of reason dispensed through the harmony of porticos, loggias, columns, pediments and domes, all set in perfect unison with each other and the nature around them.

The result is a stunning compendium of buildings across the Veneto region, most of it now designated as a UNESCO World Heritage Site. From the late 1530s until his death, Palladio built dozens of churches, villas, palazzos, palaces and country houses so forensically attuned to classical ideals that even the proportions of rooms and facades were based on mathematical ratios. Like his idol Vitruvius, Palladio consigned much of his philosophy to paper; his principal treatise, *I quattro libri dell'architettura* (*The Four Books on Architecture*, 1570), would have enormous influence on future generations.

One of its most enthusiastic audiences was in England, where Palladianism was revived twice: in the early 17th century by Inigo Jones, who used it to bring classicism to England, then a century later by young radicals like Colen Campbell and Lord Burlington, who harnessed it to purify what they saw as the egregious excess of the Baroque age. In fact Baroque, as the emotional anathema of Palladianism, was its biggest rival, and it is because of Baroque's dominance of 17th- and early-18th-century European art and architecture that Palladio's work was successively revived and reassessed.

Palladio's legacy does not endure solely in his buildings. Despite modern architecture's obsession with the glamour of the 'new', Palladio teaches us that architecture is more about reinventing old ideas than creating new ones. Ancient Rome and Greece inspired Vitruvius, who inspired Palladio, who inspired Inigo Jones, who inspired Lord Burlington; Thomas Jefferson and the architects of the New World were inspired by them all, and so on. With each generation learning from the one before, architecture, especially classicism, is defined more by cycle than by concept. There is no better proof of this than the rebranded echoes of Palladianism resounding quietly through the ages.

INIGO
JONES

ENGLAND 1573–1652

HIGHLIGHTS
Queen's House, Banqueting
House, Covent Garden Piazza

PRINCIPAL STYLE
Palladianism

ABOVE: Inigo Jones

NORMALLY, NEW ARCHITECTURAL STYLES EVOLVE SLOWLY, THE CONSEQUENCE OF LIKE-MINDED PEOPLE WORKING TO SUPPLANT AN OLD IDEOLOGY.

Towards the end of the 16th century, for example, the Roman Catholic Church essentially created the Baroque as a counter-Reformation cultural movement that was gradually ingrained into European society by an army of painters, sculptors, artists and architects. Rarely does someone single-handedly introduce a new style to a reluctant host country with one building. But that's exactly what Inigo Jones did.

His Queen's House at Greenwich Palace, begun in 1619, must have appeared like an alien visitation to

BELOW: The Rubens ceiling
in the Banqueting House,
Whitehall.

BELOW: An aspect of the Queen's House, Greenwich, showing off its geometric perfection.

the startled populace. The Renaissance was well over a century old, and classicism had replaced Gothic as *de rigueur* for European society long before Jones was born. But England, engorged on Tudor nostalgia and anti-Catholic suspicion, had clung to its older Jacobean, Elizabethan and Gothic styles. So when the Queen's House landed with its perfect symmetry, whitewashed walls, level roofline and sash windows, it heralded a cultural revolution that would change the face of Britain.

Jones revelled in disruption. Born in humble London surroundings to a Welsh cloth worker, he initially worked as a set designer. Here he was introduced to the glamour of court life and rose through the ranks to become chief designer of elaborate theatrical performances ('masques') for King James I and his long-suffering wife Anne of Denmark. During his life Jones staged over 500 of these and introduced two innovations that revolutionized English theatre production: movable scenery and the proscenium arch.

But it was his impact on architecture that would soon be more keenly felt. By 1613 his creative expertise was such that he was appointed surveyor to the king's works, effectively responsible for all royal construction. He took a tour of Rome and northern Italy, where the work of Palladio deeply affected his architectural outlook. The Queen's House, with its precise proportions and geometric simplicity, owes a clear debt to Palladio – an affinity Jones instilled into all his subsequent work.

His next project, the Banqueting House of 1622 – part of the rambling Whitehall Palace – was arguably his greatest built work and continued his campaign to embed the Renaissance in England. With its monumental Palladian double-height façade and spectacular internal hall crowned by a sublime allegorical fresco by Peter Paul Rubens, Jones outdid the Queen's House in scale and ornamentation and showed that his one-man mission to classicize England had the firm approval of his enlightened royal patron.

Jones returned to Whitehall in 1638, when James's son Charles I was king, to produce plans to pull down the building (except the Banqueting House) and rebuild it as a spectacular Renaissance palace. With seven stupendous courtyards and stretching the half mile from present-day Northumberland Avenue to St. James's Park Lake, this colossal classical structure would have cemented Charles I's absolutist ambitions and transformed central London. Unfortunately those ambitions were cut short by the English Civil War, which culminated ironically in the king being executed at the very Banqueting House that was to be the crux of his palatial masterpiece.

Jones had better luck elsewhere. He added a classical portico to Gothic St. Paul's Cathedral in London, though both were destroyed in the Great Fire fourteen years after his death. He designed a number of country houses, most famously Wilton House in Wiltshire, its magnificent Double Cube Room (1653) combining Palladian proportions with sumptuous gilded decoration. Jones was also proficient in town planning and left an indelible imprint on central London, designing houses (1641) and a largely unrealised plan for its oldest and largest square, Lincoln's Inn Fields.

Covent Garden Piazza (1630) matched the Queen's House for groundbreaking innovation as the country's first formal classical square. Inspired by Italian models and overlooked by continuous identical elevations, it was perfectly symmetrical, uncharacteristically formal for London and centred on a fine porticoed church which Jones also designed. It revolutionized London town planning and inspired the panoply of residential squares that now define the city.

Jones's legacy is immense. Though the Civil War cut short his work, and the country turned to Baroque when the monarchy was restored eleven years after King Charles's death, Jones had the last laugh when the Palladianism he championed was established as England's signature style for the first half of the 18th century. The architects who orchestrated that changeover, Lord Burlington, Colen Campbell and William Kent, were all heavily influenced by Jones. Undoubtedly England's greatest Renaissance architect, he will be remembered as the man who brought classicism to England and dragged the country kicking and screaming into the modern age.

LEFT: 17th century engraving of Covent Garden Piazza.

GIAN LORENZO
BERNINI

ITALY 1598–1680

HIGHLIGHTS
St. Peter's Square and
Colonnades, Sant'Andrea al
Quirinale, Fontana dei Quattro
Fiumi

PRINCIPAL STYLE
Baroque

ABOVE: Gian Lorenzo Bernini

AN ARTIST OF THE FIRST ORDER, BERNINI CREATED SOME OF THE BEST EXAMPLES OF BAROQUE ART AND ARCHITECTURE MADE IN THE SERVICE OF CATHOLICISM. HOWEVER, HIS VOLATILE PERSONALITY MADE HIM AN UNLIKELY INSPIRATION FOR MORAL INSTRUCTION, BUT PERFECT FOR UNDERSTANDING THE DRAMA OF THIS STYLE.

Towards the end of the 16th century, the Catholic Church, terrified and appalled by the Reformation, created a visually opulent art movement that would amplify the glory of God and distract from the spiritual failings exposed by Martin Luther and others. The Baroque movement remains one of the most successful political makeovers in history, dominating the arts across Europe and beyond for much of the next two centuries.

This is why the tumultuous life and dysfunctional family of Gian Lorenzo Bernini, the greatest architect of the Baroque age, presented a problem to a religious patron intent (at least ostensibly) on probity. Handsome, passionate and gifted, Bernini was proclaimed a child prodigy just eight years after his birth in Naples, following in his father's footsteps and excelling at the profession in which he initially found fame: sculpture.

RIGHT: Colonnades around St Peter's Square, Rome.

BELOW RIGHT: The dramatic Baroque ceiling of Sant'Andrea al Quirinale.

Bernini could be tempestuous and spiteful. In his thirties, when he discovered that his married lover was also involved with his younger brother, he flew into a rage, almost killing his brother and arranging for his mistress's face to be mutilated. Years later, when his brother brutally sodomized one of Bernini's young assistants, Bernini himself defended the crime by persuading Queen Christina of Sweden (an illustrious client) to testify in court that sodomy was common among Neapolitans in Rome. Although Bernini later repented and found redemption in marriage and

faith, his passionate temper was a perfect reflection of the Baroque style he embodied. Baroque derives from the Portuguese *barroco*, which means uneven or damaged pearl. The translation sums up the Baroque perfectly: beautiful yet broken, a celebration of the flawed rather than the formal.

Baroque was all the things that strict, hermetic classicism was not. It gleefully drove a coach and horses through classical doctrine in the pursuit of power, melodrama and theatre. Baroque architecture recruited every dramatic device known – movement,

monumentality, contrast, colour, illusion, light, shade, ornamentation, three-dimensionality – to mount a vehement spatial assault on the senses that demanded an emotional response from the breathless onlooker.

This is what Bernini's work provided. His sculptures were ceaselessly expressive, hyper-naturalistic renditions of the human form frozen in dramatic poses and encased in flowing robes to intensify the sense of movement. These themes culminate in his most famous sculpture, the *Ecstasy of St. Teresa*, officially a figurative portrayal of a nun in the throes of religious ecstasy but alleged by generations of scandalized scholars to represent ecstasy of an altogether more corporal kind.

These same principles electrified his architecture. In his greatest work, St. Peter's Square (1656-67) in Rome, Bernini encloses his sprawling square in a pair of monumental colonnades that extend like arms around the religious faithful. In true Baroque tradition the gesture is carefully sequential and utterly theatrical; the colonnades begin as a curve before pinching suddenly outwards to follow perspective as they hurtle towards the final act of Carlo Moderno's stupendous façade to St. Peter's Basilica. With its gigantic scale, spatial shifts and carefully choreographed geometric movements, it remains one of the greatest pieces of Baroque architecture and town planning ever conceived.

Bernini designed churches, chapels, fountains and squares in the same manner, generally adding to or remodelling others' work but emblazoning each with his signature energy. Virtually all his commissions were in Rome, and Bernini did much to mould its Baroque character. His prolific patron Pope Urban VIII told him, 'You are made for Rome and Rome was made for you.'

Bernini's greatest rival was another towering Baroque genius, Francesco Borromini. Where Bernini could be charming and ebullient, Borromini was truculent and melancholic and ended his life by killing himself with his sword at sixty-seven. Despite despising each other, they both worked on one defining project that encapsulates Bernini's architectural genius.

In the 1650s, Pope Innocent X transformed the Piazza Navona into one of Rome's most spectacular public spaces. Bernini's centrepiece, *Fontana dei Quattro Fiumi* (Fountain of the Four Rivers), features a massive pile of marble, travertine and granite supporting a soaring replica of an Egyptian obelisk. The seraphs and deities Bernini carved into the fountain clamber around a rocky plinth that spews water into the surrounding pool; one figure uses his arm to theatrically shield his gaze from the awesome spectacle of Borromini's Sant'Agnese in Agone church opposite.

In this gesture we find the essence of Bernini. His fountain was conceived not as an inanimate, autonomous, decorative object but as a dramatic humanistic response to its surroundings, the euphoric climax to a Baroque set-piece that linked architecture, public space, statuary and water into a dazzling operatic whole. As an architect, sculptor, artist, painter, dramatist and urban planner, Bernini understood how all art, especially Baroque, was about the total sensuous experience and that architecture without emotion was nothing.

LEFT: Fontana dei Quattro Fiumi (Fountain of the Four Rivers).

RIGHT: Detail of a horse within the fountain's centre.

LOUIS
LE VAU

FRANCE 1612–1670

HIGHLIGHTS
Louvre Colonnade, Palais de Versailles, Collège des Quatre-Nations

PRINCIPAL STYLE
Baroque

ABOVE: Louis Le Vau

SEVENTEENTH-CENTURY FRANCE WAS EUROPE'S CULTURAL EPICENTRE AND THE WORLD'S SOLE SUPERPOWER, WITH PARIS THE WORLD'S LARGEST CITY. FRENCH ARCHITECTURE WAS THEN DOMINATED BY TWO PEOPLE: JULES HARDOUIN-MANSART AND LOUIS LE VAU.

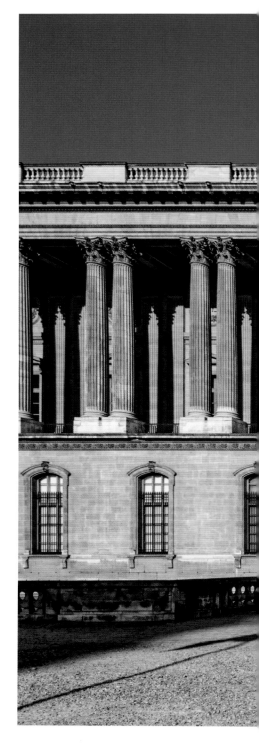

ABOVE: The Louvre Colonnade.

Both worked directly for the powerful King Louis XIV, giving them the opportunity to shape the image and identity of France.

Hardouin-Mansart (1646–1708) was responsible for some of Paris's most famous buildings (Les Invalides church) and public spaces (the showcase squares of Place de Victoires and Place Vendôme). His masterpiece was the expansion of the royal palace of Versailles, remodelling and extending the garden wing completed by Le Vau just before the latter's death. Hardouin-Mansart also created the spectacular Hall of Mirrors that has helped cement Versailles as the archetypal royal palace. His work marked the high point of Baroque splendour associated with Louis XIV's court, so much so that it is sometimes called the Louis XIV style.

And yet Le Vau's work has arguably had wider cultural impact, largely because of one exceptional project: the Louvre Colonnade. Long before this, Le Vau had charted a successful career. Born to a Paris stonemason, he initially worked with his father and

younger brother. He was designing town houses for the aristocracy when he came to the king's attention, eventually landing the lucrative commission to design the chateau for the king's superintendent of finances.

In many ways Vaux-le-Vicomte (1658–61) is the archetypal French Baroque chateau. With its tall hipped roof and pronounced vertical elevational accents, it follows the tradition of French Renaissance classicism, broken only by the decadent intrusion of the near-futuristic central dome. More importantly for Le Vau's career, it powerfully synthesizes the triple formal conditions of landscape, architecture and interior; in working with the celebrated landscaper André Le Nôtre and the renowned court

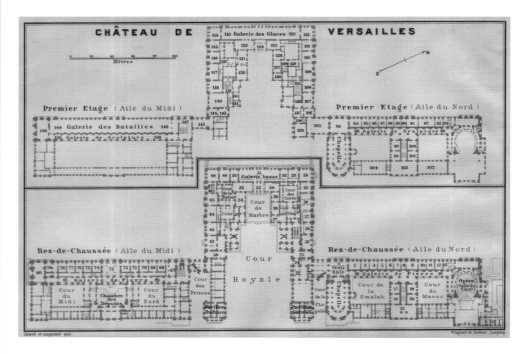

CHÂTEAU DE VERSAILLES

Premier Etage (Aile du Midi)

Premier Etage (Aile du Nord)

Rez-de-Chaussée (Aile du Midi)

Cour Royale

Rez-de-Chaussée (Aile du Nord)

LEFT: A plan of the layout of the Palace at Versailles.

BELOW: The domed central block of the Collège des Quatre-Nations.

RIGHT: Though the Hall of Mirrors at Versailles was designed by Jules Hardouin-Mansart, it would not have been possible were it not for Le Vau's monumental expansion of the building from a hunting lodge to a royal palace.

painter Charles Le Brun, Le Vau formed a successful partnership that would be repeated at Versailles.

Louis XIII had purchased Versailles as a small hunting lodge before enlarging it into a modest chateau. His son Louis XIV had ambitions to turn it into a sublime dynastic palace, and from 1661 on, Le Vau was hired to do it. He cleverly retained the chateau as the core of a greatly expanded complex that now overlaid its Renaissance host with formal, classical elevations above an arched and rusticated plinth. While Hardouin-Mansart expanded the palace and added its showcase interior, Le Vau designed the key garden front elevational template which Hardouin-Mansart multiplied to such tremendous effect.

Other royal commissions followed, including remodelling the south wing of the Louvre's central courtyard, and the spectacular Collège des Quatre-Nations (1662-88) which, with its curving symmetrical wings extending from a massive domed central block, owes much to the dynamic geometric choreography of Italian Baroque. It is easily Le Vau's most Baroque design.

This sits rather strangely with his greatest work, the Louvre Colonnade (1665-74). Several esteemed architects were invited to tender designs for it. Bernini spent months in Paris for this purpose, returning to Rome enraged that none of his designs were selected. His rejection shows the growing confidence of French

classicism against the previously dominant cultural benchmark of Italian Baroque.

Le Vau did not design the winning entry alone but was the senior party in a team including fellow architect Claude Perrault and again Le Brun. The design is remarkable for its cool restraint and monumental clarity. Gone are the contorted histrionics of the Baroque and the mansard roofs of the French Renaissance. Instead there is a simple, severe, almost diagrammatic elevational arrangement that sees softly projecting central and side accents set around two magnificent, deeply recessed twin-column colonnades surmounted by a continuous balustrade. As a composition it was well ahead of its time, anticipating the neoclassical revival and Beaux-Arts movement of the 18th–19th centuries. It helped set the standard compositional and decorative template for public buildings across the world, such as the Place de la Concorde palaces, Garnier Opera House, Metropolitan Museum of Art, Pennsylvania Station, and even the side wings on the US Capitol Building. Le Vau did not just create a new façade for a former royal palace, he helped create one of the most influential buildings in Western architecture.

CHRISTOPHER WREN

ENGLAND 1632–1723

HIGHLIGHTS
St. Paul's Cathedral, Greenwich
Hospital, Hampton Court Palace
(South & East wings)

PRINCIPAL STYLE
English Baroque

ABOVE: Christoper Wren

WHEN CHRISTOPHER WREN WAS BORN, ENGLAND WAS CONSIDERED A CULTURAL BACKWATER. FRANCE UNDER LOUIS XIV WAS EUROPE'S CULTURAL LEADER, AND MOST EUROPEAN COUNTRIES TENDED TO ADAPT FRENCH AND ITALIAN STYLES.

England was no different, for centuries absorbing Romanesque, Gothic and Palladian styles and modifying them to suit Anglo-Saxon tastes. The thought of English architecture influencing anywhere else was laughable.

By the time Wren died, London had been transformed. It had the second-largest classical dome in Christendom, had in St. Paul's Cathedral arguably Britain's most internationally influential piece of architecture ever, had Europe's greatest collection of

BELOW: St Paul's Cathedral is a touchstone on London's skyline.

RIGHT: The Painted Hall at Greenwich, known as Britain's Sistine Chapel.

Baroque churches outside Rome, and had the English version of the Sistine Chapel at Greenwich Hospital. English architecture was now a coveted cultural export to Europe and beyond, and one man was largely responsible for this astonishing turnaround. He remains the greatest architect Britain has ever produced.

Wren was born to a respected clergyman and his wife in rural Wiltshire a decade before the English Civil War. He designed his first building at thirty-one, the chapel at Pembroke College. Before this Wren was a scientist, mathematician and astronomer, and this grounding gave him a technical competency and an appreciation for meticulousness, rationality and problem-solving that would serve him well in his later career.

Wren's shift to architecture came with two seismic events in his life: a trip to Paris in 1665 and the Great Fire of London the following year. With Versailles and the Louvre being expanded, Paris was a hive of construction, and Wren encountered the Baroque style he eventually adopted. While there is no record of him meeting Bernini, who was in Paris at the time competing for the Louvre commission, the Italian's presence signifies the intensity of Baroque influence that Wren would inevitably have witnessed.

That influence became apparent after the Great Fire. Never one to miss an opportunity, within a week Wren had drawn up plans to rebuild chaotic, irregular London as a gleaming metropolis of arrow-straight avenues radiating from a gridded array of formal piazzas. The plans were staggeringly ambitious, but despite enthusiastic backing from King Charles II,

landowners refused to shift from their plot leases. But the fire had lit the Baroque fuse, which came gloriously alight with the only part of the plan to be fully realized: St. Paul's (1675-1711).

The cathedral, including Inigo Jones's great Renaissance portico, had been destroyed in the fire, and Wren and the king immediately planned its reconstruction. Wren's favoured plan, which survives in the Great Model now displayed in the crypt of the cathedral, shows the effect of Paris on Wren and the maturity that his approach to Baroque had already attained. Based on the more centralized (and Baroque) Greek cross floor-plan, rather than the Latin cross favoured by Gothic cathedrals, St. Paul's was conceived as a vast pedimented classical temple surmounted by a Baroque dome similar in scale to St. Peter's.

That was a problem. Post-Reformation England was a place of religious sectarianism, and the idea of its principal church mimicking the architectural rituals of Baroque Catholicism was anathema to Church authorities. They dutifully approved an alternative design Wren had produced strictly for appeasement, a nonsensical anglicized hybrid of Gothic and classical with a spire instead of a dome. That it was never built is testament to Wren's tactical and political aptitude. With the king's tacit support, he exploited the contractual capacity the Church had given him to make 'ornamental variations', varying the design entirely to build the utterly unrelated building we see today.

St. Paul's is a masterpiece, but it is also a very English compromise. Built to a Latin cross plan and complete with hidden flying buttresses, it conceals its Gothic compliances behind the classical dress Wren favoured. With its enormous scale, monumental aspect, rich ornamentation, expressive statuary and unforgettable dome, it is also undoubtedly Baroque. But Wren forged a compromise that was more tempered than its Italian counterparts and emphasized qualities like spatial dynamism and structural complexity. The English Baroque was born.

It was a style Wren made popular in England for the next half-century. After becoming surveyor to the king's works in 1669, he amassed an astonishing array of achievements. In the thirty-six years it took to build St. Paul's, he somehow also built Kensington Palace, Greenwich Hospital, Greenwich Observatory, and the Royal Hospital Chelsea, half of Hampton Court Palace, several new buildings for Oxford and Cambridge colleges, and palatial mansions, Temple Bar's ornamental archway, the Monument to the Great Fire and, perhaps most impressively, fifty-two Baroque City of London churches that brought a distinct architectural identity to England's fledgling Anglican church.

This extraordinary body of work reveals Wren's versatility, ingenuity and creativity. No two buildings are the same; his later projects at Greenwich and his sadly unbuilt plans for Whitehall Palace in particular show a Baroque compositional inventiveness that matched Bernini's. Like Bernini, Wren understood the importance of the totality of art and wisely collaborated with gifted sculptors, painters, woodcarvers and ironmongers to embellish his buildings with the ornamentation required to create the sensory experience that Baroque demanded.

By the end of Wren's life, Baroque had been expunged in England by a resurgent Palladianism, whose adherents made clear their embarrassment at what they saw as the riotous emotional extravagance of St. Paul's. But Wren's legacy lives on: in the many domes inspired by St. Paul's, from the Pantheon in Paris to the US Capitol; in St. Petersburg, created as a facsimile of the church domes and spires that Peter the Great saw on a 1698 visit to London; and in the work of the many architects Wren inspired. It lives on especially in the example he set of how architecture must use the canniest art form of all: compromise.

OPPOSITE ABOVE: An interior view from St Paul's Cathedral.

RIGHT: The Fountain Court at Hampton Court Palace designed by Wren.

NICHOLAS
HAWKSMOOR

NONE OF THE ENGLISH BAROQUE ARCHITECTS INFLUENCED BY WREN WAS MORE MAVERICK, ENIGMATIC AND PERHAPS GIFTED THAN HIS PUPIL, NICHOLAS HAWKSMOOR – THOUGH FOR CENTURIES HAWKSMOOR'S LEGACY WAS UNFAIRLY MEASURED ONLY IN REFERENCE TO OTHER ARCHITECTS.

ENGLAND 1661–1736

HIGHLIGHTS
Christ Church Spitalfields, Easton Neston, Westminster Abbey Towers

PRINCIPAL STYLE
English Baroque

ABOVE: Nicholas Hawksmoor

Wren recruited him as a young clerk upon hearing of his skill, giving him an assistant's role on some of the greatest works of the day, including Greenwich Hospital and Kensington Palace. Hawksmoor later assisted Sir John Vanbrugh on his two masterpieces, Castle Howard and Blenheim Palace.

This deferential relationship with England's two leading Baroque architects has obscured the fact that Hawksmoor had a genius that matched and sometimes surpassed their own. There is also the fact that Hawksmoor's life, like his buildings, existed in shadows. Not much is known about it before he came to work for Wren at eighteen. He was born in Nottinghamshire shortly after the monarchy was restored, and his humble background may also have constrained his posthumous appreciation.

Hawksmoor, unlike the mannerly Wren and debonair Vanbrugh, was said to be quiet and pensive, prone to dark moods and prolonged introspection – characteristics evident in his architecture. But his

LEFT: Staircase in the manor house, Easton Neston.

RIGHT: Christ Church with its imposing spire in Spitalfields.

works are infused with such eccentric originality and re-inventive brilliance as to render them unique in the pantheon of British architecture.

Though many of his buildings were designed collaboratively, later he built much by himself, and from these projects we can learn most about his approach. In 1711 Queen Anne, a deeply devout woman, passed the *Fifty New Churches Act for the Cities of London and Westminster*, partly as a means of morally cleansing London neighbourhoods marked by dissipation and vice. Of the fifty proposed churches, only twelve were built, and six were by Hawksmoor, between 1712 and 1731.

The churches see Hawksmoor's uncompromising and unorthodox Baroque at its height. They are impressively monumental, intensely dramatic and contain the pediments, porticoes, arches and columns that form the accepted tenets of classicism. But these elements are obscenely exaggerated with monumentality – not necessarily expressed by the scale of the building but by the juxtaposition of massive stone elements and smaller incisions. At St. Mary Woolnoth, heavy rustication suggests a compressive quality that alludes to an even weightier mass, while tiny windows punched into thick walls and surmounted by oversized keystones point to a savage and sinister volumetric subversion of the conventional illusory conceits in which Baroque usually delights.

But it is the spectacular Christ Church Spitalfields, arguably Hawksmoor's greatest church, that fully reveals the unconventional potency of his work. With its soaring pyramidal spire, aggressive sculptural quality and massive shafts of bare, undecorated stonework, it has a raw, almost geological violence, as if chiselled from a single mighty rock. Its thrusting rib-like projections, interspersed by deep, hooded voids, combine with a cleanly pointed silhouette to give the church a mystic, Gothic quality as much Pagan altar as Christian church. Sepulchral and sacrificial, ethereal and otherworldly, Christ Church Spitalfields retains a brooding tension and an atmospheric oppression that mark a darkly virtuoso interpretation of the Baroque far removed from the elegant precision of Wren.

Not all of Hawksmoor's work was this funereal. At his Clarendon Building Cambridge, elements of the King William Block at Greenwich Hospital and the sadly incomplete Easton Neston country house, he

LEFT: The heavy rustication of St. Mary Woolnoth.

ABOVE: The mausoleum at Castle Howard.

resorted to the more conventional Roman temple model, albeit enlivened by his dramatic interplay between solids and voids and his powerful assembly of solemnly unadorned stone volumes.

The enduring legacy of his superb churches, along with the haunting beauty of his mausoleum at Castle Howard, ensures that Hawksmoor's architecture has puzzled and captivated generations of writers, artists, poets, filmmakers and even occultists. Indeed, a cult of personality has grown up around him: 20th-century popular culture repeatedly associated him, probably unfairly, with all manner of perverse folkloric ritualism, from Jack the Ripper to Satanism. One of the more lurid observations is that if one joins the dots of Hawksmoor's London churches on a map, it reveals a shape that resembles the Eye of Horus, an Ancient Egyptian hieroglyph that can be variously interpreted as a symbol of good health or the land of the dead. Apocryphal or not, it is indicative of an architect whose extraordinary buildings captured a rare and timeless sense of poetry and spirituality that remains powerfully resonant to this day.

JOHN
VANBRUGH

ENGLAND 1664–1726

HIGHLIGHTS
Blenheim Palace, Castle Howard, Greenwich Hospital

PRINCIPAL STYLE
English Baroque

ABOVE: John Vanbrugh

DURING A TIME WHEN ARCHITECTS OFTEN PURSUED MULTIPLE PROFESSIONS, SIR JOHN VANBRUGH WAS THE ULTIMATE POLYMATH.

A longside being arguably the key exponent of his era's English Baroque triumvirate, comprising Wren, Hawksmoor and himself, Vanbrugh was at times a playwright, political activist, property developer, theatre impresario, naval officer and prisoner.

Other than his architecture, Vanbrugh is chiefly remembered as a dramatist: his play *The Provoked Wife* is still regularly in production across the world. This duality is additionally interesting, for in his

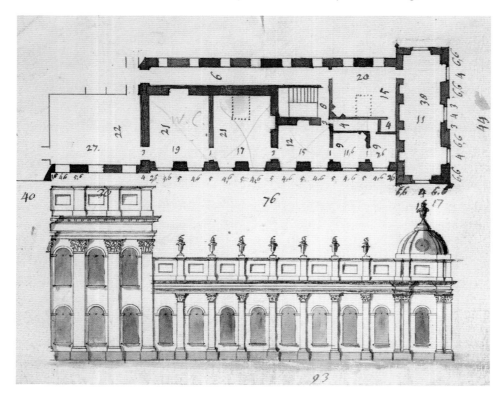

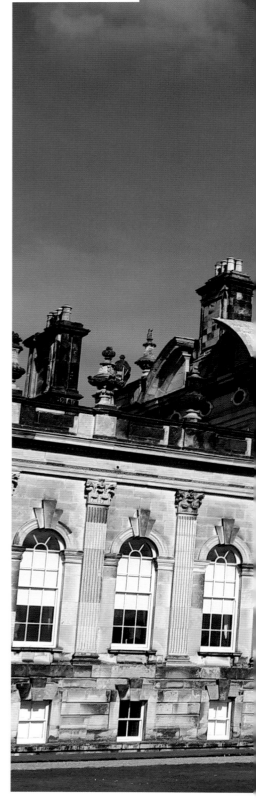

architecture and eventful life we see the same elements of theatricality and performance.

Vanbrugh was the fifth of an amazing twenty children, the son of a Flemish-Protestant cloth merchant whose faith would influence Vanbrugh's own political beliefs. In the febrile 1680s Vanbrugh somehow became a secret agent working to overthrow Catholic James II in favour of the future William III, a Protestant. Here he reveals himself to be a committed member of the Protestant Whig political faction, later a key source of patronage.

Vanbrugh's alleged sedition saw him arrested in Calais in 1688 and jailed for four years. Upon his release he spent a short time in Paris, which had a formative impact on his architectural career. Exposure to recently completed works like the Louvre and Les Invalides gave him a taste of how ostentatious architecture could be manipulated for an emotional response.

This characteristic was abundantly clear in Vanbrugh's first building, when at thirty-six he turned his hand to architecture. Helped by his Whig connections, he won the commission to build the new country seat of the Earl of Carlisle, beating the surly William Talman to the job. Thus, Castle Howard (1701-09) was born. It was to change Vanbrugh's career and English architecture forever.

England had never seen anything like it. Chatsworth House was already in construction, and Wren had been building in the Baroque style for decades. But theirs, at least initially, was a more strictly classical Baroque, whose Catholic excesses were tempered for an English audience. At Castle Howard, Vanbrugh forced a more extravagant Baroque to roar into life, dripping with an infusion of decadence, statuary and ornamentation. In its sumptuous domed entrance hall, we find the greatest interior Vanbrugh ever designed and see the prosaic rituals of domestic life transformed into a riotous spatial opera of colour, scale and monumentality.

If it is drama we see at Castle Howard, then it is full-throttled melodrama we find at his greatest work, Blenheim Palace (1705-22). In its vast great court, Vanbrugh assembled architecture on a colossal urban scale. Each interlocking block has its role in a meticulously scripted piece of architectural theatre, from the colonnaded understudy side wings to the dramatic crescendo of the magnificent central portico. Along the way a supporting cast of arches,

BELOW: A panoramic view of Blenheim Palace.

RIGHT: The King William block at Greenwich Royal Naval College, done in partnership with Nicholas Hawksmoor.

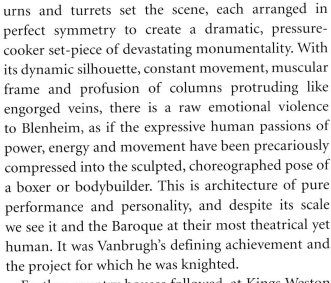

urns and turrets set the scene, each arranged in perfect symmetry to create a dramatic, pressure-cooker set-piece of devastating monumentality. With its dynamic silhouette, constant movement, muscular frame and profusion of columns protruding like engorged veins, there is a raw emotional violence to Blenheim, as if the expressive human passions of power, energy and movement have been precariously compressed into the sculpted, choreographed pose of a boxer or bodybuilder. This is architecture of pure performance and personality, and despite its scale we see it and the Baroque at their most theatrical yet human. It was Vanbrugh's defining achievement and the project for which he was knighted.

Further country houses followed, at Kings Weston (1719) and Seaton Delaval (1728), but Vanbrugh would never reach those heights again. He came closest with his completion of Wren's Greenwich Hospital, and his additions to the King William block (1702) –

achieved with his friend and long-term professional partner Hawksmoor – reveal some of Blenheim's raw, compressive monumentality.

Vanbrugh's is a life of contradictions. With no formal architectural training, he created some of the greatest works of English architecture. An avowed Protestant, he designed buildings charged with the exuberance of Catholicism. Even his personal life presents a paradox: despite writing bawdy plays that depicted marriage as a licentious romp, he did not marry until he was fifty-five, and by all accounts maintained nuptial bliss until his death seven years later.

If there is any consistency in Vanbrugh's life, it is his innate understanding of a core human trait – drama. Whether in script or on stone, Vanbrugh brought drama to life, and in his incredible architecture we do not just see it but can touch it too.

JOHN NASH

THROUGHOUT LONDON'S LONG HISTORY, ONLY ONCE DID THE CITY'S IRREGULAR, ORGANIC PATTERN TOLERATE THE IMPOSITION OF A SINGLE, GRAND URBAN PLAN.

UNITED KINGDOM 1752–1835

HIGHLIGHTS
Buckingham Palace, Regent Street, Marble Arch

PRINCIPAL STYLE
Neoclassicism / Regency

ABOVE: John Nash

Wren tried in vain in 1666, but 150 years later another architect succeeded, doing more to shape the look and character of central London than any architect except Wren himself.

John Nash was a leading figure of the British neoclassical movement that replaced Palladianism in the mid-18th century. Born in south London to a Welsh millwright, and engaged at fifteen as an apprentice to eminent architect Robert Taylor, he soon grew tired of his Palladian master's strict classical rules.

LEFT: Though the main frontage of Buckingham Palace was completed by others, it remains Nash's most famous work.

ABOVE: Today London's Regent Street and Piccadilly Circus are much altered but Nash was responsible for their original layout and design.

England yearned for something that subscribed to the general rules of classical antiquity as conveyed through Vitruvius's ubiquitous prism. But it also sought something freer, lighter and more dramatic than the forensically controlled hegemony of Palladio, something that was not just devised for elegant villas but could also be applied to the bigger public buildings of the Industrial Revolution. Western culture yearned for grandeur, not just grace. And so the neoclassical movement was born.

Nash's initial contributions to it were sporadic and largely unsuccessful. Bankrupt and disgraced at thirty-one after failed property speculations, he fled to Wales. More ruinous still was his first wife with her mountainous debts and fake pregnancies. Returning to London twelve years later, Nash acquired two things that would transform his life and the course of British architecture: a new wife, who soon became mistress to the Prince of Wales, and hence a friendship with the future king that would form arguably the

most successful public–private partnership in British architectural history.

The Prince Regent, later George IV, was decadent, dissolute and debauched. But he was also a paragon of fashion, style and taste, and arguably Britain's finest royal patron of arts and architecture. From 1806 until his death, Nash had the enviable task of turning London from a rambling Renaissance capital into a great metropolis worthy of its status as the hub of the largest empire the world had ever seen.

Central to this plan was *Via Triumphalis*, a grand imperial way that eventually stretched from Buckingham Palace to the newly formed Regent's Park – the only formal, large-scale urban plan ever successfully realized in London. It is striking how many familiar buildings and public spaces Nash's vision was responsible for: Regent Street, Piccadilly Circus, Trafalgar Square, Waterloo Place, Regent's Park, Regent's Canal, Marble Arch, Theatre Royal Haymarket, Clarence House, Carlton House Terrace and Buckingham Palace.

Buckingham House was a 1703 Baroque mansion purchased by King George III as a private family retreat in 1761. Such modesty was unacceptable to George IV, who instructed Nash to rebuild it on an imperial scale. While the current palace is much altered, its core remains Nash's U-plan configuration and sumptuous suite of state apartments, which endures in public consciousness as the definitive benchmark for opulent domesticity.

Nash's trademark Regency style, named after his patron, was the last permutation of the Georgian style established in Britain with the resurgence of Palladianism. It adhered to classical forms but emphasized refinement, elegance and ornamentation. Nash's buildings are neoclassical but softened with playful and idiosyncratically applied elements such as domes, turrets, spires and statuary, as well as the distinctive creamy stucco he deployed on exteriors. Unlike the era's other great British neoclassicist, John Soane, Nash did not labour over details, being more interested in his buildings' cumulative effect.

Never is this more evident than on his spectacular Regent Park terraces (1821-33). Here we see

Nash's other passion: his devotion to picturesque romanticism. Nash had been exposed to the Picturesque movement while in Wales. This aesthetic movement essentially called for architecture to work closely with nature to create beauty; it was also intertwined with the Romantic ethos that would dominate Victorian art and literature and revive Gothic architecture.

Accordingly Nash designed Gothic castles, re-landscaped St. James's Park from formal Baroque gardens to a naturalistic backdrop, and at his Brighton Pavilion forged a fantastical orgy of onion domes and minarets that paid homage to the mystic romanticism of the Far East. But by setting his creamy palatial terraces against the rich natural landscape of Regent's Park, and by devising the magnificent Quadrant to negotiate the shift in axis along Regent Street, he ensured that London's most monumental townscape aspects were humanized and dramatized by juxtaposition with idealized, naturalistic scenography.

Nash had his detractors. Some of George IV's unpopularity rubbed off on him and, though genial, he had a reputation for guile and dissemblance – defamations probably disseminated by jealous rivals. He died debt-ridden in Cowes after falling ill soon after the death of his beloved patron five years earlier.

Nash's towering legacy in the canon of architecture and town planning is clear, and proven in an unlikely place: Paris. When the future Napoleon III was in exile in London in the 1830s, he marvelled at the terraces of Regent's Park and the West End, and these eventually inspired the mighty boulevards he and Haussmann cut through Second Empire Paris 30 years later. Thanks to Nash's energy and vision, one of the most unplanned of all capital cities helped to shape one of the most planned.

BELOW: The domes and minarets of Brighton Pavilion bringing the skylines of the East to England.

JOHN
SOANE

ALONG WITH HIS GREAT RIVAL JOHN NASH, SOANE IS A TOWERING FIGURE OF BRITISH NEOCLASSICAL ARCHITECTURE.

UNITED KINGDOM 1753–1837

HIGHLIGHTS
Bank of England, Dulwich Picture Gallery, Sir John Soane Museum

PRINCIPAL STYLE
Neoclassicism

ABOVE: John Soane

While he built much less than Nash, and much of his work has sadly been demolished, history has judged Soane the more academically accomplished of the two. Certainly his work retains a meticulousness of detail, a spatial inventiveness, a deft originality and a lean decorative fluency that helped define the neoclassical period and continues to hold a particular attraction for modern audiences.

Soane was born to humble beginnings in Reading and as a young trainee architect was exposed to the practices of three of the most prolific neoclassical British architects of the period, George Dance the Younger, Henry Holland and the great Sir William Chambers, who enabled him to win a royal travel scholarship in 1778. For the next two years Soane, like many of his contemporaries, embarked on a Grand Tour to the ancient sites of Italy that would have a lasting impact on his architecture.

Upon his return he endured a sustained period of failed commissions that abated only in the mid-1780s, when he began to establish himself with a number of country house alterations. His luck truly changed in 1788, when the friendship he had formed with Prime Minister William Pitt's uncle on his travels helped win him the defining commission of his career and the project he would work on until shortly before his death almost half a century later: the Bank of England.

In the Bank of England, Soane created some of the greatest neoclassical interiors in Europe. The bank had been founded by William III in 1694 as the world's first central bank, and over his life Soane completely

rebuilt and expanded the building into the vast island complex it is today. He erected a superb suite of often domed banking halls, each one normally top-lit due to the building's enormous footprint. Each hall reveals Soane's skillful deployment of bare arches, subtle daylighting and highly controlled decoration to create a chaste yet highly modelled classical interior which lays bare the intricate interplay between light, volume, solid and void.

Much of Soane's work at the bank was demolished in the 1920s and 1930s to make way for a competent, if somewhat stolid, rebuild by modern classicist Herbert Baker. But thankfully Soane's greatest addition to the bank survives, the spectacular iconic screen that runs the full extent of its perimeter. This is a work of colossal classical confidence and control, a mighty yet supremely elegant neoclassical fortification whose huge windowless expanse appropriately exudes impenetrability yet is carefully enlivened by the rhythmic articulation of punched openings, heavy rustication and majestic screens of ornate recessed ionic columns. It is Soane's masterpiece and helped form the classical template that was applied to countless bank buildings across the world over the next 150 years.

Much of the approach employed for the bank is evident, on a smaller scale, in Soane's other work. And much of his work was also marked by an

extraordinary stylistic dexterity that proves he was very much a visionary of his time. At Pitzhanger Manor (1804) and his Soane Museum (1812), both built as his homes, he displays a rapturous devotion to Grecian antiquity. And yet at Dulwich Picture Gallery (1815) and St. John's Church in east London (1828), he creates classical boxes so shorn of decoration as to appear almost modern. Soane may have been a neoclassicist, but for him surface was always more important than style.

Soane was also very much a visionary when it came to architectural illustration. For much of his career he was fortunate enough to work with the great artist Joseph Gandy, who depicted many of his projects, built and unbuilt, as ravishing romantic ruins or surrounded by Arcadian landscapes.

Despite his genius, Soane spent much of his long life paranoid and embittered, sentiments likely exacerbated by a prolonged period of bad luck after his Grand Tour, and by his poor relationship with his eldest son, who defamed him in print and attempted to protect his inheritance by seeking to legally prevent his father from bequeathing the Soane Museum to the nation. But Soane's legacy lives on, not only in the travel scholarship his will donated to the Royal Institute of British Architects, which still runs to this day, but in those pioneering premature glimpses he gave us into what would eventually become modern architecture.

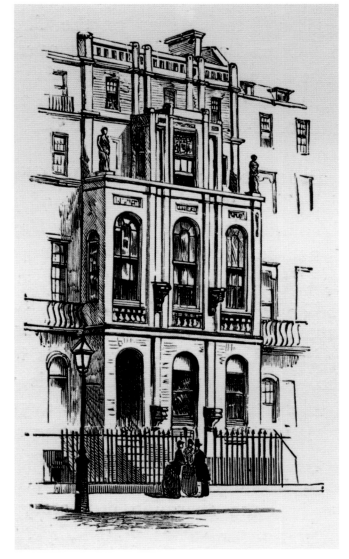

GEORGE GILBERT

SCOTT

GEORGE GILBERT SCOTT WAS PROBABLY THE WORLD'S FIRST GLOBALIST ARCHITECT.

UNITED KINGDOM 1811–1878

HIGHLIGHTS
St. Pancras Station, Albert Memorial, Foreign & Commonwealth Office

PRINCIPAL STYLE
Gothic Revival

ABOVE: George Gilbert Scott

ABOVE: The gothic spires and red brick of St Pancras Station.

Beyond designing the majority of his 800+ buildings in the UK, Scott was responsible for major works in Germany, South Africa, Canada, New Zealand, China and India. But it is not for his extraordinary internationalism that he is chiefly remembered, but for embodying the movement that is synonymous with the Victorian age and shaped vast amounts of the buildings it produced: the Gothic Revival.

Scott's hero was the tragic Augustus Welby Pugin, the driving force behind the Gothic Revival in England from 1835, when he co-designed the new Houses of Parliament as the definitive neo-Gothic building of the age with classicist Charles Barry. The revival had been percolating across Europe since the late 18th century but gained particular traction in Victorian England when it was harnessed as a convenient cultural vehicle to assert religious piety, growing imperial power and a romanticized idea of nationhood inspired by the chivalric values of the medieval age. But in 1852 Pugin committed suicide at just forty years old, and the Gothic Revival found a reluctant new hero in Scott.

Despite being one of thirteen children born to a poor Buckinghamshire clergyman and his wife, Scott, through hard work and determination and without a formal architectural education, grew to establish the largest architectural practice in Victorian England of the mid-19th century. As was typical with Gothic Revival buildings, most of his work was churches, and Scott's commissions gave life to the Victorian obsession with puritanical virtue and the pre-Reformation ecclesiasticism.

Accordingly, practically all of Scott's religious buildings feature the medieval Gothic detail one would expect, such as prolific use of the pointed arch, rose windows, pinnacle spires, gable ends and a strong emphasis on verticality. But Scott was a fastidious innovator who also incorporated more up-to-date variations from the Victorian age, such as the use of red brick and wooden galleries, the mixing of various Flemish, Byzantine and Florentine neo-Gothic styles and the deployment of new industrial construction processes.

So much so that some allude to a certain coldness in Scott's religious Gothic, a mechanistic rigour that, while efficient, lacks the spiritual warmth of its

ABOVE: The West front of the Foreign Office, Whitehall, London, after 1873. Viewed across a lake from St James's Park.

medieval precedents, or for that matter Pugin. On his best ecclesiastical work, however, such as his re-fronting of the North Transept of Westminster Abbey (1880–90), St. Mary's Cathedral Edinburgh (1874–79) and Hamburg Nikolaikirche (1845–80, briefly the tallest building in the world), Scott displays exceptional use of the core precepts of the Gothic style.

Controversially for some Gothic Revivalists at the time, Scott believed passionately that Gothic should not be reserved solely for religious buildings, and some of his best work emerged when he applied the style to secular functions. Among the finest examples of this are his Albert Memorial (1862–72), a glittering, High Victorian reincarnation of a medieval shrine, his University of Glasgow main building

(1870) and arguably his masterpiece, St. Pancras Station (1868–73).

St. Pancras remains one of the UK's greatest examples of the High Victorian Gothic. In its vast scale, its sumptuous medieval detailing and, most impressively, its riotously romantic roofscape of spires, chimneys and pinnacles, Scott successfully recasts the Gothic style as a fantastic modern public building. Internal innovations included concrete floors, fireproofing and revolving doors. The building shares a trajectory with one of the other highlights of Scott's career, his Foreign and Commonwealth Office on London's Whitehall (1868–73). Not only does this sumptuous classical pile show an extraordinary level of stylistic dexterity for a Gothic architect, but

LEFT: A view looking up at the top of the Martyr's Memorial, commemorating the 16th Century Oxford Martyrs, which was designed by Scott and built from 1838-43.

ABOVE: The elaborate decorative touches around, and the dramatic spire atop, the Albert Memorial were typical of the Gothic Revivalist movement.

in reusing his original proposal for the scheme at St. Pancras when a Gothic Foreign Office was rejected, Scott displays the ideological pragmatism that helped galvanize his incredible success.

That success lived on long after Scott's death, for he sired an architectural dynasty that changed the face of Britain. His son John Oldrid Scott was a prolific church architect; his grandson Giles Gilbert Scott designed Liverpool Anglican Cathedral, Battersea Power Station, Bankside Power Station (now Tate Modern), Waterloo Bridge and the iconic K-series red telephone boxes; his great-grandson Richard Gilbert Scott made significant additions to London's Guildhall; and Scott's great-niece Elisabeth Scott was one of the most important female architects of the mid-20th century.

DANIEL BURNHAM

UNITED STATES

1846–1912

HIGHLIGHT
Flatiron Building, Union Station Washington DC, Rand McNally Building

PRINCIPAL STYLE
Beaux Arts

ABOVE: Daniel Burnham

DANIEL BURNHAM WAS NOT THE FIRST GREAT AMERICAN ARCHITECT. IN THE LATE 18TH AND EARLY 19TH CENTURIES, THOMAS JEFFERSON, BENJAMIN LATROBE AND CHARLES BULLFINCH HAD ALL HELPED DRIVE AMERICA'S ASTONISHING TRANSFORMATION FROM REVOLUTIONARY COLONY TO INDEPENDENT NATION, AND ALL LEFT THEIR MARK ON AMERICA'S ACROPOLIS, THE US CAPITOL IN WASHINGTON DC.

Subsequently, the great Henry Hobson Richardson ingeniously Americanized the Romanesque style.

But Burnham was the first American architect to begin defining an architectural style that was uniquely American, not just an amalgamation of European, particularly English and French, styles. Yes, Burnham was a strong exponent of the Beaux Arts tradition which came to dominate US architecture from the mid-19th century until the First World War. But in contributing to the influential first Chicago School of architecture, in masterplanning several US cities, in patenting US department-store design and, perhaps most dramatically, in co-creating the world's first steel-framed skyscraper, Burnham helped establish American architecture as a proud and distinct cultural force of its own.

Born in New York State, Burnham moved to the city he would make his own at the age of eight. It was in Chicago that he gained his first role as a draughtsman, but before that he undertook a remarkable variety of professions, including druggist, window salesman, gold prospector in the Wild West, and a run for the state legislature – showing the experimentalism and entrepreneurialism that would define his highly successful future career as an architect, into which he finally settled at the age of twenty-six.

In 1873 Burnham and his friend John Root opened a practice together that over the next decade became synonymous with the Chicago School, an architectural

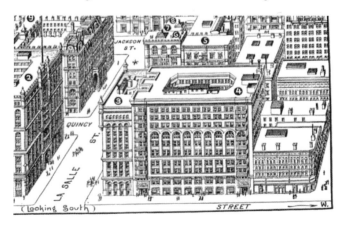

LEFT: The Rand McNally building plans; the building itself was pulled down in 1911.

RIGHT: The narrow profile of the Flatiron building in New York.

style in the city preoccupied with steel-frame construction and high-rise commercial buildings, loosely reflecting the fledgling Modernism movement in Europe. They built the 130 metre (426.5 feet) tall Montauk Building in 1886 and made history when their 140 metre (459 feet) Rand McNally Building (1890) became the tallest steel-frame skyscraper in the world. The following year, Root died tragically of pneumonia, leaving Burnham at the head of what had become the largest architectural practice in the US.

For some time before Root's death, Burnham had been working on what was the probably the defining commission of his career, the 1893 World's Fair. The tradition of world fairs had begun with England's Great Exhibition of 1851, and the Chicago exposition was to be the largest the world had ever seen. Planned on a colossal scale, Burnham designed great domed Beaux Arts classical buildings, set apart by monumental boulevards, verdant gardens and glistening lakes.

While the fair proved hugely influential on corporate America, who demanded buildings that evoked its rationalized neoclassical monumentality for decades to come, Burnham's great rival, the inveterate Modernist Louis Sullivan, was less generous, dryly (and incorrectly) predicting that 'the damage wrought by the World's Fair will last for half a century from its date, if not longer'. There is no small degree of stylistic bias and professional chagrin in Sullivan's words, as his career never hit the commercial heights of Burnham's. But in attempting to paint Burnham as a classical sycophant, Sullivan mischaracterized him as an ideologue rather than a pragmatist. For Burnham embraced the Beaux Arts aesthetic where appropriate but was always happy to combine it with all manner of modernistic intervention when necessary, as his skyscrapers proved.

This aptitude is demonstrated by much of Burnham's later work. New York's Flatiron Building (1902), arguably his most famous skyscraper, precariously squeezes an Italianate palazzo on to a narrow triangular wedge and, by utilizing a steel frame, is able to extrude it up to a dizzying 22 storeys. Burnham also reinvented the department store as a modern American consumerist symbol, designing scores of Beaux Arts emporiums across the country and beyond (including Selfridge's in London in 1909) and introducing highly successful innovations such as internal atria and large ground-floor shopfront windows – with Sullivan again dismissively maligning him as a 'colossal merchandiser'.

Burnham was a prolific urban designer too, creating city plans for Chicago, Washington DC, San Francisco and even Manila in the 1900s that all subscribed to the City Beautiful movement of rational, landscaped order and were hugely influential in promoting the principle of controlled urban growth across the US and beyond for decades to come. Culturally, the 16th century belonged to Spain, the 17th to France and the 19th to Britain. Burnham laid the architectural foundations that ensured the 20th century was the American century.

LEFT: The imposing interiors of the Grand Union Station in Washington DC.

BELOW: Selfridges in London is one of the scores of Beaux Arts emporiums that Burnham designed.

ANTONI GAUDÍ

EVERY NOW AND THEN A GREAT ARCHITECT COMES ALONG WHO IS AN ECCENTRIC, ENIGMATIC GENIUS WHO TOTALLY DEFIES CLASSIFICATION.

SPAIN 1852–1926

HIGHLIGHTS
Sagrada Familia, Casa Milà, Parc Güell

PRINCIPAL STYLE
Modernism

ABOVE: Antoni Gaudí

Some consider Gaudí an exponent of Catalan Modernism; others, a subscriber to Spanish Art Nouveau. Some have even referred to him as an advocate of High Victorianism, Modernist Baroque or, more esoterically, organic mysticism. The truth is that Gaudí had elements of all these allegiances, but there was one characteristic that defined all his work: his own immutable, idiosyncratic, imaginative, inventive and unapologetically individualistic style. His works have also become synonymous with Catalan identity and have contributed greatly to the character of Barcelona, the city that was both his home and his muse.

Antoni Gaudí was born in or near Reus in Catalonia, north-east Spain. As a child he was afflicted with a delicate constitution which plagued him with health issues he would suffer all his life. Spending long stretches of his childhood resting at the family's summer house, he reportedly spent hours contemplating the trees and landscapes and forming the strong connection to nature that would become a defining characteristic of his architecture. Later he was an inconsistent but gifted student at Barcelona's School of Architecture, where the director in 1878 provided a sign of Gaudí's artistic idiosyncrasies, wondering whether he had awarded a degree to 'a madman or a genius'.

Gaudí began his career designing elaborate Art Nouveau lampposts and newsstands for public spaces in Barcelona. Art Nouveau was an international style originally developed in Britain in the 1880s as a highly

ABOVE; Sagrada Familia, the unfinished cathedral that was Gaudí's masterpiece.

organic and naturalized variant of the Arts and Crafts movement, and as such it was perfectly aligned with Gaudí's naturalistic sympathies. It is also evident in his first major project, a house for a Barcelona brick and tile manufacturer in which we first see Gaudí's indomitably unorthodox architectural spirit emerge.

Casa Vicens (1883) is half-gingerbread-cake, half-building, a flamboyant, colourful, tile-encrusted villa emblazoned with a cusped loggia and gift-wrapped in woven ribbons of patterned ceramic tiles. The ingrained eclecticism that Gaudí would exhibit throughout his career is evident in the variety of influences at play, principally Art Nouveau, Moorish and nature, all colliding in a twisting, kaleidoscopic, almost maniacal orgy of colours, materials, profiles and patterns. This rich mix of stylistic influences continued throughout Gaudí's career, and he was routinely inspired by Gothic, Oriental and, in his later years, hyper-naturalistic decoration and forms, the latter evident on the cave-like beehives that are

Casa Milà (1906–12) and the reconstructed Casa Batlló (1904–6).

Casa Vicens set the distinctive theme for Gaudí's subsequent buildings, many of which were commissioned by his most enthusiastic patron, Catalan industrialist Eusebi Güell. The projects he compiled for Güell are some of his masterpieces; his Parc Güell (1914) and Colònia Güell (1898–1914) in particular show Gaudí at the height of his naturalism and playfulness, crafting wistful, dream-like structures infused with riotous colours, organic forms and daringly improbable parabolic geometries.

Beyond Gaudí's trademark naturalistic affinity and stylistic eclecticism, two elements primarily defined his work: religious symbolism and structural and material representation. Both came to sublime fruition on his greatest work, Sagrada Familia basilica. Throughout his life Gaudí was a deeply religious man; he died, with great ignominy, dishevelled and unrecognized after being hit by a tram on his way to evening vespers at the age of seventy-four. He designed a number of chapels and churches throughout his career, but none occupied him to the extent of the famously unfinished church he worked on from 1883 until his death.

Sagrada Familia is an illusory, illogical and utterly inspirational masterpiece that, like its creator, defies classification. Part Gothic, part organic and with conical, pockmarked towers and rugged, cliff-face facades, it presents itself to the outside world as a sculpted heap of rough-hewn, sugar-coated masonry.

LEFT: The entrance to the fantastical Parc Güell.

ABOVE: A view from above of Casa Milà, one of the apartment buildings that show Barcelona's architectural debt to Gaudí

RIGHT: Window detail from Casa Batllo, Gaudí's other stunningly unique apartment building.

Inside, with its colourful forest of spindly piers leaning up towards a carved, vaulted ceiling, we see a church interior exhilaratingly cast as a vast celestial grotto.

Yet there is method to Gaudí's apparent madness. He had spent years perfecting structural equilibrium, the theory of structure standing alone with no support, like a tree. By understanding the thrusts and forces acting upon them and compensating by manipulating geometry, materials and scale accordingly, Gaudí could make his structures bend, lean, ripple and swerve like strings being plucked on a guitar. For all Gaudí's embryonic naturalism, it is a uniquely Modern and expressive approach to structural utility. And in his remarkable unfinished basilica, it forms a fitting memento to Spain's greatest architect.

LOUIS HENRY SULLIVAN

UNITED STATES

1856–1924

HIGHLIGHTS
Wainwright Building, Guaranty Building, Carson Pirie Scott Building

PRINCIPAL STYLE
Modernism

ABOVE: Louis Henry Sullivan

CREDITED AS ONE OF THE FOUNDING FATHERS OF MODERNISM, LOUIS SULLIVAN IS WIDELY CONSIDERED TO HAVE CREATED THAT MOST AMERICAN OF ARCHITECTURAL FORMS: THE SKYSCRAPER.

BELOW: The Wainwright building in St Louis, Missouri, encircled with more modern skyscrapers.

Through doing so, he helped establish the first Chicago School as a hotbed of late-19th and early-20th-century architectural and engineering innovation, catapulting the young city to international fame and appointing it as the spiritual home of the skyscraper long before Chicago's 1892 height limit effectively handed the title to New York.

Sullivan is also renowned for penning one of the most famous architectural aphorisms of all time and the ideological mantra for the whole Modernism movement: 'form follows function' – though he gallantly attributed it to Vitruvius. Accordingly, Sullivan influenced scores of future Modernist architects in both Europe and the US, most notably his protégé, Frank Lloyd Wright.

It was clear that Sullivan was an architectural prodigy from his youth. Born to Swiss-Irish immigrants in Boston, he entered the illustrious Massachusetts Institute of Technology at just sixteen. After a year he moved to Chicago, attracted by the building boom sparked by the Great Chicago Fire of 1871. He eventually became a partner in the firm where he would work for most of the rest of his life, Adler and Sullivan.

Sullivan's preoccupation with high-rises was part of a wider trend that had been gaining strength in Chicago since Elisha Otis invented the passenger lift in 1857 and made tall buildings feasible for the first time. The development of steel at affordable prices in the second half of the 19th century was also critical, as this helped foster and finance a new kind of structural solution where an internal steel frame could help the external walls bear the load of a building.

Despite Sullivan's nickname 'the Father of Skyscrapers', what is generally considered the world's first skyscraper, Chicago's Home Insurance Building of 1885, was attributed to William Le Baron Jenney. Equally, Chicago's tallest buildings at the time, the Montauk and McNally Buildings (the latter became the tallest steel-frame skyscraper in the world), were built by Sullivan's great Chicago rival, Daniel Burnham.

But Sullivan takes precedence in the annals of skyscraper folklore – not because he was the first to build them, or because his skyscrapers were the tallest, but because his buildings powerfully and poetically

evoked the innate spirit of skyscraper design. Sullivan's tall buildings, such as St. Louis's Wainwright Building (1891) and Buffalo's Guaranty Building (1896), were strident and soaring expressions of verticality, using columns and unbroken punched bays that would extend continuously up to nine or ten storeys to cast the eye upwards in the manner of a pointed Gothic arch.

With the external facade freed from its load-bearing responsibilities by the internal steel frame, Sullivan developed a new elevational language liberated from the structural constraints of historical styles. He thereby created, as his aphorism goes, a simpler, clearer and more honest external expression of internal (structural) function. In the

revolutionary aesthetic licence that this allowed, we find the seeds of Modernism.

A core misinterpretation of later Modernists inspired by Sullivan's work was that in his celebration of structural and volumetric clarity and simplicity, he had rejected ornament. This rejection formed a central tenet of Modernism and was a cause of much controversy and cultural resentment in later years. And it was based on a fundamental misunderstanding of Sullivan's work.

After moving to Chicago in his youth, Sullivan had trained at the famous École des Beaux-Arts in Paris. While he was never an ideological subscriber to the style, unlike Burnham, it did give Sullivan a

grounding in the power of decoration, to which he remained enthralled for the rest of his life. So while Sullivan's buildings often exhibit a stark monolithic severity, they were carefully embellished with ornamentation in a vivid variety of materials. This ranged from the elaborately embossed cast-iron reliefs on Chicago's Rothschild Building (1881) to the spectacular eruption of quasi-masonic decorative cartouche stonework around the entrance of the otherwise spartan Merchants' National Bank (1914) in Grinnell, Iowa.

Equally, by vertically stacking his tall buildings into three volumes of base, centre and top, and using subtle ornamentation to differentiate between them, Sullivan was mimicking the vertical arrangement of the archetypal hybrid of structure and decoration: the classical column. Like Vitruvius and Palladio before him, and unlike many of the Modernists who followed him, Modernism's founding father was prescient enough to understand that progress is as much a question of repackaging the past as it is of rejecting it.

FRANK LLOYD WRIGHT

UNITED STATES
1867–1959

HIGHLIGHTS
Fallingwater, Johnson Wax HQ, Solomon R. Guggenheim Museum

PRINCIPAL STYLE
Modernism

ABOVE: Frank Lloyd Wright

IT IS NOT HYPERBOLE TO CALL FRANK LLOYD WRIGHT THE GREATEST AMERICAN ARCHITECT TO DATE.

Over half of the thousand or so structures he designed during an astonishing seventy-three-year career were built, and four were listed by the 2000 American Institute of Architecture Convention among the ten greatest buildings of the 20th century, with Fallingwater at the top. Not only did his work revolutionize American architecture and help cement Modernism as the default 20th-century style, it also had a profound and unprecedented influence on European Modernism and inspired the likes of Willem Dudok, Walter Gropius and the De Stijl art movement. Such was Wright's fame that, unusually for an architect, he has seeped into popular culture and his life has been immortalized in a play, an opera and a song.

Part of Wright's genius was his ability to work in a huge variety of Modernist sub-movements while retaining a distinctly American vernacular and expressing his own inimitable style. That style centred on a close relationship with nature, a fearless approach to material innovation and a relentless pursuit of geometric purity. That said, the fact that it is almost impossible to reconcile futuristic buildings like Guggenheim (1943–59) and Johnson Wax (1936–39) as being designed by the same architect who completed Tudor and Queen Anne-style houses in his youth is testament to his extraordinary ingenuity and dexterity as an architect.

ABOVE: Fallingwater, considered one of the greatest buildings of the 20th century.

LEFT: Another view of Fallingwater within its green grounds.

Wright was a Modernist in the sense that his buildings maintained a rigorous functional clarity, and as a youth he worked in the office of his idol and early mentor, Louis Sullivan. But he infused his Modernism with a warmth and intimacy that did not eschew ornamentation or prolific use of natural materials, particularly on the interiors of the multiple houses he designed. Wright was a famously proud and recalcitrant authoritarian figure whose tempestuous life included infidelity, two divorces, seven children and an employee murdering seven people at his Iowa home.

Beyond Sullivan, Wright barely admitted to being influenced by anyone other than himself. But he did have great respect for that other scion of Modernism, Ludwig Mies van der Rohe, and he also professed to be inspired by Japanese art – an affinity that is evident in his Willits House (1901) and elements of his seminal Robie House (1910), both in Chicago.

The Prairie School, of which Wright was a pioneer, was arguably the Modernist sub-movement with which he was most associated and for which he compiled some of his most iconic works. The school was a Midwestern variant of the Arts and Crafts movement and sought to wrest domestic design away from European influence and forge a new American residential vernacular inspired by native prairie landscapes. We see it at its pinnacle in two of Wright's greatest houses, Robie House and the spectacular Fallingwater (1935) in rural Pennsylvania.

In their strident linearity, tectonic solidity, deeply overhanging eaves and swooping horizontal forms, Wright presents perhaps the most sublime renditions of the compositional control, geometric simplicity and sculpted massing that defined his style and makes both buildings appear astonishingly ahead of their time. With Fallingwater cantilevered precariously over a gushing waterfall, and its slabs of horizontal concrete darting outwards as if organically expelled from the rocky ravine behind it, we see Wright achieving the most stirringly symphonic synthesis between architecture and nature of his career.

Yet he completely changed tack for his iconic Johnson Wax HQ in Wisconsin, shifting from prairie whisperer to sci-fi innovator. Here the masterpiece is the Great Workroom, a vast open-plan office where forests of thin lily-pad columns shoot up to a translucent ceiling formed by Pyrex tubing, the first time the material had been used in this manner. The Pyrex tubes then curve where they meet the walls to make it appear as if the columns are improbably supporting nothing but a glowing celestial orbit. Structurally ambitious and futuristically organic, this spectacular space seems to belong to the 21st century rather than the start of the 20th.

As does Wright's last great project, New York's Guggenheim Museum (1959). Here, well into his eighties, Wright reinvents himself yet again as a curatorial expressionist, redefining a museum space as a whitewashed ramped promenade encased in a sliced concrete spiral shell that again seems voluptuously organic and shockingly ahead of its time. Intensely personal and soulfully enigmatic, Guggenheim neatly summarizes Wright's legacy: that of a relentlessly gifted and quintessentially American innovator who harnessed nature to humanize Modernism.

LEFT: The voluptuous curves of New York's Guggenheim Museum

BELOW: Work area within the Johnson Wax Headquarters building.

CHARLES RENNIE
MACKINTOSH

UNITED KINGDOM 1868–1928

HIGHLIGHTS
Glasgow School of Art, Hill House, Willow Tea Rooms

PRINCIPAL STYLE
Art Nouveau

ABOVE: Charles Rennie MacKintosh

WIDELY RECOGNIZED AS SCOTLAND'S GREATEST ARCHITECT, CHARLES RENNIE MACKINTOSH IS STILL REVERED IN HIS NATIVE GLASGOW.

The fire in 2018 that virtually destroyed his most famous project, the Glasgow School of Art, caused an outpouring of civic grief in the city. This strong affinity with Mackintosh's work is partly prompted by the fact that his architectural style was so unmistakably personal to him and intimately concerned with the totality of the work of art. As well as the buildings themselves, Mackintosh would design curtains, chairs, lights, door handles, windows, tables, bookcases and cabinets, establishing a rigorous thematic consistency that unified his architecture and transformed it into brand as well as building.

BELOW: Adornment detail on the Scotland Street school shows the style made famous by Mackintosh.

RIGHT: The entrance to the Willow Tea Rooms.

The Glasgow School of Art

Born into a middle-class Glasgow family, Mackintosh was the fourth of eleven children but, as a result of the crippling child mortality rates of the day, one of only seven to survive infancy. He developed an early interest in architecture and, at the age of twenty-two while at the Glasgow School of Art, he came second in a student travelling scholarship named after the great Glaswegian neoclassicist architect Alexander 'Greek' Thomson and designed to further the study of classical architecture.

But it was designs of a more exotic kind that chiefly caught Mackintosh's attention. Glasgow's position on the River Clyde and its 19th-century industrial status as a great shipbuilding and seafaring city meant that it was particularly exposed to international influences. Those influences were most keenly exerted by Japan, whose imperial navy purchased a warship built in Clyde shipyards in 1889 and with whom Glasgow enjoyed increased trading links.

Mackintosh was immediately drawn to the clinical restraint and streamlined efficiency of Japanese art and was heavily influenced by it throughout his professional life. He combined this with an adherence to the organic naturalism of Art Nouveau and an appreciation of the heavy-set cones and curvatures of Scottish baronial architecture. The rich stylistic plurality created by this eclectic mix is what came to define Mackintosh's work.

But it was also characterized by something altogether more esoteric and enigmatic: Mackintosh's distinctive personal style. His architecture and particularly his interiors are almost instantly recognizable by his compendium of trademark features. The use of his adored floral decorative motifs, stained-glass windows, spaces discreetly subdivided by screens, the juxtaposition of gentle curves and angular forms, the atmospheric expressionism of heavy dark materials framing narrow slits of diffuse light, high-backed chairs carved into ornamental panels, decoration that is restrained rather than ostentatious – all these are the signature stylistic flourishes embedded into Mackintosh's work.

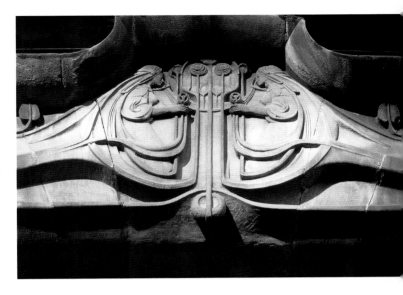

ABOVE: Figurative sculptural detail from entrance of the Glasgow School of Art.

Nowhere are they more ebulliently expressed than in the Glasgow School of Art he attended and then rebuilt between 1896 and 1909. It is the definitive Mackintosh work. Its subtly asymmetrical stone facades reject Beaux Arts monumentality and revel in whimsical Art Nouveau flourishes like shallow arches, slit windows, stunted turrets and skirted volutes. The interiors are pervaded by a humble domestic simplicity and a methodically decorated functionality throughout, with the prolific use of wood on beams, balustrades, columns and walls making the building resemble a large yet intimate single piece of furniture. These themes culminate in the showcase library, where the minimalist ornamental angularity makes the Japanese influence clear. The school represents the pinnacle of Mackintosh's career, although simultaneous projects like Hill House (1904) repeat the internal themes but encase them in a chaste baronial shell.

Despite a long and happy marriage to a wife he met while a student and who, as an artist, collaborated with him on several projects, Mackintosh died in London aggravated by drink and depression and disillusioned with architecture. But a 1960s revival of interest in Art Nouveau, coupled with a growing fascination with a more intimate, humane and romantic Modernism as the style itself declined, have ensured his legacy ever since.

LEFT: Built in two phases, the Glasgow School of Art was completed in 1909. This photograph was taken c.1992 before the 2014 and 2018 fires.

EDWIN LUTYENS

ONE OF THE GREATEST BRITISH ARCHITECTS OF THE 20TH CENTURY, LUTYENS WAS ALSO NOTABLE FOR STRADDLING TWO SIGNIFICANT PERIODS OF BRITISH SOCIAL AND ARCHITECTURAL HISTORY.

UNITED KINGDOM 1869–1944

HIGHLIGHTS
The Cenotaph, Rashtrapati Bhavan, Midland Bank HQ

PRINCIPAL STYLE
Modern Classicism

ABOVE: Edwin Lutyens

The country houses and colonial commissions at the start of his career, including the colossal classical master plan and government buildings for New Delhi, spoke of the immense imperialist reach and confidence of the British Empire at its peak. Back home in Britain, this confidence was reflected in a traditional vernacular domestic architecture conspicuously designed to evoke the enduring cultural ideal of English rural repose.

Then, after the seismic global shock of the First World War, we see Lutyens changing tack, reverentially commemorating and immortalizing the dead in a remarkable series of war memorials across Britain and abroad. Chief among these is London's iconic Cenotaph (1920), whose solitary aspect and bare, sepulchral restraint exudes a sublime poignancy that forms arguably Britain's most poetic architectural wartime commemoration. And also, in his London department store and hotel, his seminal collection of Midland Bank buildings and even in a solitary but significant chequerboard social housing scheme at London's Page Street (1930), he deftly responds to the new commercial and social realities the Great War had left in its wake.

Along the way, Lutyens shows great stylistic versatility in shifting from the Arts and Crafts

RIGHT: : Rashtrapati Bhavan, the presidential palace in New Delhi, India.

vernacular that helped define the late 19th century to a looser, freer, more modernistic interpretation of the classicism and neo-Baroque that defined the early 20th. His work therefore acts as a dynamic architectural lens through which to view a period of severe political and socio-economic disruption and adjustment, not just for Britain but for the world.

The first stage of Lutyens' long and successful career is defined by a series of exquisitely realized Arts and Crafts private country houses. Starting with Surrey's Orchards and Munstead Wood in 1897, and stretching almost twenty houses later to the extraordinary medievalesque Castle Drogo in Devon in 1911, we see Lutyens working chiefly in the Tudor style to craft a number of idyllically conceived houses that borrow heavily from traditional rural vernaculars and styles. Innovatively composed and richly varied in both materials and articulation, the

houses were often framed by lusciously landscaped gardens and set a harmonious pastoral template that Lutyens would effectively reuse in his two churches at Hampstead Garden Suburb (1909–11).

Then everything changed. In pursuit of a grand architectural style that more fittingly reflected British imperial supremacy at the time, architects like Aston Webb and Lanchester & Rickards had established a new flamboyant Edwardian Baroque style heavily influenced by the work of Wren. But the irregular layout and tortuous planning constraints of British cities, especially London, ironically made achieving imperial urban grandeur a taxing enterprise in Britain but not in its colonial dominions. The jewel in the colonial crown was the British Raj in India,

and in 1912 Lutyens was given the once-in-a-lifetime opportunity to head a team planning its new capital, New Delhi.

Lutyens' New Delhi work marks some of the most ambitious, visionary and monumental architecture that any British architect has completed outside Britain. Executed on a giant scale that would be unthinkable in Britain, Lutyens planned a vast new government quarter centred on what remains the country's presidential palace and, in area covered, the largest residence of any head of state in the world. At Rashtrapati Bhavan, formerly Viceroy's House (1912–31), Lutyens created a gargantuan classical temple arranged around a stupendous courtyard and surmounted by a gigantic drum dome set high above

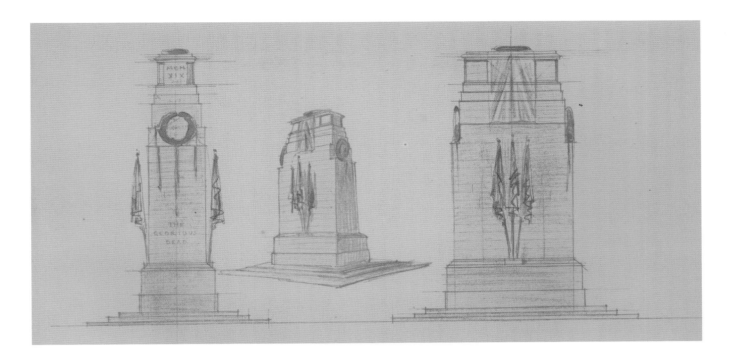

a deep recessed central colonnade. Arrow-straight avenues radiate out in four directions, connecting to other grand government buildings that Lutyens designed and his superb compendium of monumental ornamental architecture scattered around the estate, including Jaipur Column (1930) and India Gate (1931).

This is a stripped-down, coolly decorated hybrid of neoclassicism and neo-Baroque that represents a vastly compositionally inflated version of Wren's Greenwich Hospital. And yet, in its Buddhist-inspired dome and red sandstone walls, Lutyens again displays pronounced vernacular empathy by borrowing from traditional Indian architecture. The only other project he designed that came close to this scale was his spectacular design for Liverpool Metropolitan Cathedral (1933). Sadly only the crypt was ever built. Had it been completed, not only would it have had the world's largest dome and been second in size only to St. Peter's, but in its ingenious combination of Baroque, neoclassical, Romanesque and Modern, it would have demonstrated once again Lutyens' virtuoso vernacular versatility.

ABOVE: Sketch No 1 by Lutyens for the Cenotaph, Whitehall, Westminster, London.

BELOW: Cenotaph decorated in poppies for Remembrance Day.

WALTER GROPIUS

GERMANY 1883–1969

HIGHLIGHTS
Bauhaus School Dessau,
Gropius House, Fagus Factory

PRINCIPAL STYLE
Modernism

ABOVE: Walter Gropius

THE BAUHAUS SCHOOL WAS ONE OF THE MOST INFLUENTIAL MODERN ART MOVEMENTS OF THE 20TH CENTURY, AND BY FOUNDING IT, GROPIUS TAKES HIS PLACE ALONG WITH THE LIKES OF MIES VAN DER ROHE, ALVAR AALTO AND LE CORBUSIER AS ONE OF THE GREAT PIONEERS OF MODERNISM.

His spare and efficient use of steel frame and glass curtain walls also helped establish the International Style, which would revolutionize skyscraper design and transform the look and feel of city centres across the world.

Famously unable to draw, Gropius saw no difference between the artist and the craftsman and viewed design as an exercise in combining an almost intuitive sense of beauty with functional utility and streamlined industrial mass production, principles that underpinned his Bauhaus pedagogy. In so doing, his influence was able to extend far beyond architecture and into many of the domestic accoutrements facilitated by the growth in 20th-century mass consumerism, such as lamps, tables, chairs and ashtrays. Consequently, through Bauhaus, Gropius transformed his approach to design into one of the most recognizable and desirable lifestyle brands of the 20th century.

Gropius was born to a notable Prussian family and was nephew of the architect of Berlin's former

ABOVE: The Fagus Factory, a German shoe last company, whose building was commissioned by owner Carl Benscheidt.

RIGHT: The Bauhaus building in Dressau, Germany, named for the movement that Gropius founded.

Kunstgewerbemuseum. He married composer Gustav Mahler's widow after studying architecture in Munich and Berlin. After graduation, his formative architectural years were spent at the practice of famed German architect and designer Peter Behrens, where his fellow employees included Ludwig Mies van der Rohe and Le Corbusier. Gropius left Behrens to start his own practice with friend and future Bauhaus collaborator Adolf Meyer. But before Bauhaus they designed a modest shoe factory in Alfeld, Lower Saxony, that would change the face of European Modernism forever.

The Fagus Factory (1911-13) formed a three-dimensional embodiment of the core principles of early Modernism. Heavily influenced by Behrens' seminal 1909 AEG Turbine Factory in Berlin, it updated that thesis by encasing the factory in a radical structure that rejected AEG's heavy brick masonry in favour of lighter glass curtain walls. The walls are articulated to form thin brick columns that gently peel backwards as they get higher, to play a recessive, skeletal role between the more prominent shafts of glazing, thereby reflecting the internal structural frame and adhering to Louis Sullivan's legendary aphorism that 'form follows function'. So it is the glass – geometrically subdivided into smaller rectangular mullions – rather than the structure that dominates. In this radical redistribution of elevational emphasis, combined with simplified linearity, we see the seeds of what was to become the International Style.

But that was not the style with which Gropius was to be associated in perpetuity. After military service during the First World War, he was invited to become master of the Grand-Ducal Saxon School of Arts and Crafts in Weimar in 1919. Gropius almost immediately changed the name to Bauhaus (literally 'building house'), and one the most famous art movements of the 20th century was born. It was based on the principle of *Gesamtkunstwerk*, which refers to the 'totality' of the work of art, an idea that had preoccupied Bernini, Wren and Mackintosh.

Accordingly, Bauhaus sought to combine art, architecture, graphic design, pottery, ceramics and industrial design to create an artistic fusion rigorously informed by sophistication of craftsmanship, utility of function and industrialization of manufacture. Aesthetically, Bauhaus forms were influenced by clean lines, angular geometries, bold colouration and structural expressionism, elements we see very much on display in the Dessau school building that Gropius designed in 1925. These characteristics reveal the Russian Constructivist influences that were at Bauhaus's roots but not necessarily the unlikely inspiration that Gropius took from the English Arts and Crafts movement, in craftsmanship if not in aesthetics.

It is impossible to overstate the influence of Bauhaus, and therefore Gropius, on how we live today. Its visual style informed subsequent generations from as far afield as London's Barbican by Chamberlin, Powell and Bon (1965–76) and the 4,000 buildings designed in the Bauhaus spirit in Tel Aviv's White City in the 1930s. More importantly, by using Bauhaus to turn Modernist design into a consumerist commodity, Gropius gave architecture a domestic familiarity it had rarely enjoyed before.

BELOW: Model of a single family house by Gropius.

WILLEM
DUDOK

SHOWCASING HIS WORK IN HILVERSUM, WILLEM MARINUS DUDOK CEMENTED HIS REPUTATION AS THE FATHER OF DUTCH MODERNISM.

NETHERLANDS
1884–1974

HIGHLIGHTS
Hilversum Town Hall,
Vondel School, De Bijenkorf
department store

PRINCIPAL STYLE
Modernism

ABOVE: Willem Dudok

BELOW: Hilversum town hall,
by night.

B eing appointed the municipal architect of the North Holland province town of Hilversum gave Dudok the incredible opportunity to design practically all of the town's civic buildings. Over a remarkable thirty-year period, he created twenty-five housing projects, seventeen schools, two cemeteries, a slaughterhouse, a pumping station and a series of sports and recreation buildings, bathhouses and bridges. Collectively these seventy-five buildings form one of the most complete and coherent compendiums of unified Modernist architecture and urban planning anywhere in the world. His greatest building is Hilversum's spectacular

Town Hall, a breathtakingly dramatic Modernist masterpiece yet one that attains infinite harmony through its sinuous juxtaposition of mass, materials, geometry and nature.

Dudok initially sought to pursue a military career but became attracted to architecture after studying civil engineering at the Breda military academy and designing military installations for the Dutch army. After concentrating exclusively on architecture, he was eventually appointed assistant director of public works at Leiden in 1913. A promotion two years later to the position of director of public works at Hilversum paved the way to the ultimate opportunity of being appointed Hilversum's municipal architect in 1928 and charged with significantly expanding the city.

Dudok had built up a solid body of public works that revealed his personal style and influences, all of which came to fruition on his array of Hilversum works. He was heavily influenced by the twin movements of early Modernist Dutch theory, the Amsterdam School and De Stijl. The Amsterdam School worked primarily with brick and used it to create dynamic, expressionist forms and integrate the interior of a building with the exterior. De Stijl sought to create simplified abstractions of geometric forms and was intimately preoccupied with angular severity and stark, often monotone, colouring.

Both influences are clearly evident in Dudok's Hilversum works. His buildings were built mostly from brick, and while his advocacy of De Stijl generally disregarded the Amsterdam School's preoccupation with curves, projects like his Vondel School show his willingness to create expressive geometric forms based on clear horizontal and vertical lines.

Bauhaus was also a major influence, and we see this most vividly on his De Bijenkorf department store in Rotterdam (1930), sadly destroyed in Second World War bombing. Here his solid brickwork mass is variously encased in sheaths of translucent glass, and the strong 'ocean liner' horizontal articulation hints at more playful Art Deco sympathies.

This broad range of stylistic influences culminates sensationally at Hilversum Town Hall. The building is encased in brick and is conceived as an interlocking asymmetrical amalgamation of rectilinear volumes of varying width and heights. The constant kinetic shifting between each volume adds an almost seismic quality of motion and dramatic tension to the exterior, a process that reaches its climax in the soaring 48 metre (157.5 feet) tower, Hilversum's tallest structure.

Much of the building's impact comes from its stunning sculptural quality, with thin windows sliced into the envelope and a sequence of narrow fins, buttresses and incisions expressing a verticality that vies with the strong, streamlined horizontality of the dramatically overhanging rooflines. Yet the entire volatile composition is held together by a keen sense of balance and harmony, the latent power of its thrusting angles calmed by the imposition of rational, geometric order.

The Town Hall's strong linear massing owes much to Frank Lloyd Wright, whose work greatly inspired Dudok. Equally, its subtle integration with landscape, with one side of the building emerging directly from a lake, shows allegiance to Ebenezer Howard's Garden City movement, a theme Dudok introduced constantly throughout Hilversum. Therefore, as well as his stellar collection of Hilversum buildings and his sublime Town Hall, Dudok's chief legacy is to remind us though his multiple influences of Modernism's and architecture's habitual stylistic porosity.

LUDWIG MIES
VAN DER ROHE

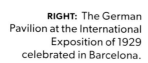

GERMANY / UNITED STATES

1886–1969

HIGHLIGHTS
Barcelona Pavilion, Seagram Building, Lafayette Park

PRINCIPAL STYLE
Modernism

ABOVE: Ludwig Mies Van Der Rohe

IF LOUIS SULLIVAN'S APHORISM 'FORM FOLLOWS FUNCTION' HELPED DEFINE THE ETHOS OF EARLY MODERNISM, THEN IT IS LUDWIG MIES VAN DER ROHE'S EQUALLY TIMELESS 'LESS IS MORE' THAT SUMMARIZES MODERNISM IN ITS MORE MATURE STATE.

Sullivan had argued in the late 19th century that ornamentation was an essential part of the Modernist credo. But, by the late 1920s, when Mies designed his seminal Barcelona Pavilion, decoration was already being quietly written out of the movement in favour of the leaner, cleaner and simpler lines Mies coveted.

At its core, Mies's eloquent minimalist mantra was based on his belief that the power of architecture lay in economy rather than excess. By radically diverting Modernism's ideological narrative towards his preferred trajectory from the 1930s onwards, and by recruiting one of the most iconic symbols of Modernism – the American skyscraper – to do it, Mies stands with Le Corbusier as the greatest figure of 20th-century European Modernist architecture and the only living architect whom Frank Lloyd Wright ever judged as his equal.

Yet it was not Modernism but neoclassicism to which Aachen-born Mies turned at the start of his career. In his early twenties he was employed as an apprentice at the practice of renowned German Modernist Peter Behrens, where he worked alongside Walter Gropius and Le Corbusier. Upon leaving, he

RIGHT: The German Pavilion at the International Exposition of 1929 celebrated in Barcelona.

set up his own practice designing neoclassical houses for the German nobility. But the trauma of the First World War as well as his grounding at Behrens soon convinced him that the old world order these homes represented had collapsed. He started experimenting obsessively with designs in the new Modernist style that he hoped would eventually become as synonymous with the new world as neoclassicism had been with the old.

His big breakthrough came when he turned these ideas into reality with his extraordinary pavilion for the 1929 Barcelona Exposition. Gone was the applied decoration and masonry solidity of neoclassicism. In its place was a simple glass and marble box whose lavish materials, swooping angular geometries, layered spatial porosity, and forensically sculptural form and detailing gave it the sheer, crystalline elegance of a glistening minimalist jewel case. Despite being torn down after the exposition closed, the building caused a sensation and almost immediately shifted the Modernist debate in Mies's minimalist direction. Faithfully reconstructed in 1986, it remains one of the

highlights of his long career and is one of the most important buildings in the history of Modernism.

With Mies's reputation as a Modernist pioneer now established, he continued to practise but suffered from dwindling commissions after the Great Depression and the collapse of the Weimar Republic. Also, while serving as the last director of the Bauhaus School at the request of former colleague and Bauhaus founder Gropius, he was subject to increased harassment from a Nazi regime hostile to the progressive utilitarianism that Bauhaus and Modernism preached. Reluctantly he emigrated to America in 1937, but this marked the beginning of the most fruitful period of his career.

Based in Modernism's spiritual home of Chicago, over the next three decades Mies became arguably the leading practitioner of the International Style, a major subset of Modernism that prioritized sharp rectilinear forms, volumetric clarity, sheer plane surfaces, almost total reliance on the core industrial materials of steel, concrete and glass, and a complete lack of ornament – in short, a pure architectural expression of the minimalist sympathies that Mies demonstrated at Barcelona.

Mies applied the style to scores of buildings in the US and abroad, several of which were the skyscrapers with which he and the style became synonymous. Perhaps the most famous is his seminal 38-storey, 157 metre (515 feet) Seagram Building in New York of 1958. Arguing that the external expression of the internal structural frame could compensate for the lack of applied decoration, Mies mimicked the internal structure (which fire codes prevented him from exposing) on the exterior elevations by totally encasing the skyscraper in a curtain wall grid of extruded, bronzed non-load-bearing steel beams and mullions separated by infill glazing.

This arrangement set the default diagrammatic elevational tone for commercial high-rises in city centres across the world for the next half-

LEFT:: The towering Seagram Building, New York.

ABOVE: The 1959 78-acre Lafayette Park residential district in Detroit, USA set a benchmark for large-scale Modernist urban renewal.

RIGHT: An interior view from the German Pavilion, which was faithfully reconstructed in the 1980s.

century. Few of these buildings matched Seagram's quality, and the banal monotony that this template induced when indifferently applied was responsible for much of the reaction against Modernism when it fell to its inevitable decline in the 1970s. But in the stripped simplicity and tectonic purity of Mies's best work, we surely see an architectural rendition of the spiritual beauty he alludes to in the second aphorism he made famous: 'God is in the details.'

LE CORBUSIER

SWITZERLAND / FRANCE 1887–1965

HIGHLIGHTS
Villa Savoye, Unité d'habitation, Chandigarh Palace of Assembly

PRINCIPAL STYLE
Modernism

ABOVE: Le Corbusier

WITH HIS TRADEMARK HORN-RIMMED GLASSES AND SILK BOW-TIE, LE CORBUSIER WAS NOT ONLY THE DEFINITIVE EXPONENT OF THE MODERN ARCHITECTURE MOVEMENT BUT ALSO ONE OF THE MOST ICONIC FIGURES OF THE 20TH CENTURY.

The sculptural expressionism and near-puritanical functionality of his works killed the romance of decoration for good, and provided the ideological template which drove Modernism throughout the mid-20th century and inspired its later Brutalist phase. His veneration of concrete in all its forms made it Modernism's signature material and created a popular and unprecedented public association between the

BELOW: Villa Savoye, which embodies Le Corbusier's Five Points of Architecture.

movement and the material that endures to this day. And as a town planner obsessed with the technological sanctity of the home and the organic organization of the city, Le Corbusier held theories of urban residential redevelopment that would have enormous influence on towns and cities across the globe.

And yet, even today Le Corbusier remains a deeply controversial and divisive figure. He famously described houses as 'machines for living in', and while this dictum clearly appeals to the functional efficiency he and Modernism so craved, it effectively stripped homes (and often their residents and by extension their cities) of their humanity. Thus brutalized, it became easier to assemble the mass public housing schemes of the 1960s and 1970s whose tower blocks and totalitarianism had devastating social consequences and which still often stand in cities across the world as spiteful scions of Modernism's eventual downfall.

Le Corbusier's initial interests were more aligned to philosophy, art and architectural writing, and it was while writing for the journal he founded in

Paris in 1920 that he indulged in the nomenclatural trend favoured among Parisian avant-gardes at the time and dispensed with his birth name of Charles-Édouard Jeanneret in favour of the more ambiguously iconoclastic Le Corbusier. Throughout the 1910s and 1920s Le Corbusier had slowly assembled an architectural body of work, mainly on private houses. But it was not until 1928 that he received one of the defining commissions of his career: Villa Savoye, just north-west of Paris.

The villa embodies Le Corbusier's Five Points of Architecture, which he had been developing through his various books and writings in the 1920s. It was supported on pilotis (thin columns), had long horizontal windows for light and air, had a flexible interior devoid of load-bearing walls, had a facade entirely unconstrained by structure and was topped with a functional roof configured as a garden. While not strictly one of his five points, the building was also expressed as the unadorned white concrete box that would evolve into his signature form. Villa Savoye was hugely influential on both Modernism and its later International Style variant, and the principles it established would underpin much of Modernist theory for almost the next half century.

Over much of the next four decades, Le Corbusier amassed an extraordinary portfolio of groundbreaking Modern buildings that would revolutionize cities and architecture around the world. In the 1950s, arguably his creative peak, he designed a number of stunning, ethereally charged religious buildings, most famously his exceptional, mushroom-topped Notre-Dame du Haut (1955) in eastern France, which stands as one of the most whimsically organic commissions of his career. The 1950s also saw his collaboration with talented young Brazilian architect Oscar Niemeyer on the iconic United Nations HQ in New York (1952), which helped to establish the podium and slab arrangement that defined high-rise buildings across the world for the rest of the century. Also during this period he was invited to design the new Indian city of Chandigarh, where he crafted a remarkable assembly of Modernist civic buildings that stand as one of the most complete large-scale examples of Modernist architectural and urban theory anywhere in the world.

Le Corbusier's urban and residential theories are the most problematic when assessing his legacy. He was undoubtedly charged by genuine reformist zeal to improve on the overcrowded urban slums bequeathed by the 19th century. But as is so often the case, realization failed to match intent. In a series of mercifully unbuilt functionalist urban visions, he prepared for future utopian cities in the 1920s and in the oppressive scale and composition of his defining Unité d'habitation housing in Marseilles (1952), we see Le Corbusier pursuing the ultimately futile task of trying to mechanize and automate humanity. He is to be commended for attempting to bring rationality into a disordered world. But in glorifying the machine over the user, Le Corbusier unwittingly unleashed a new generation of nihilistic inhumanity in mid-20th-century housing and urbanism that would inflict great social damage on the world he sought to heal.

LEFT: Rooftop terrace view of the relaxation area at Unité d'habitation with the nursery school and the children's pool.

BELOW: Notre Dame du Haut completed in 1955.

PAUL REVERE
WILLIAMS

UNITED STATES
1894–1980

HIGHLIGHTS
LAX Theme Building, Las Vegas Guardian Angel Cathedral, Ad Astra Estate

PRINCIPAL STYLE
Modernism

ABOVE: Paul Revere Williams

IT IS THE NATURE OF ARCHITECTURE TO UNIFY AND HUMANIZE, OR AT LEAST IT SHOULD BE. SO IT COMES AS AN UNPLEASANT SURPRISE WHEN THIS BENIGN INTENT IS CONFRONTED WITH THE COLD PREJUDICE OF RACIAL SEGREGATION.

Working as an African American architect in an era of political persecution and the endless struggle for civil rights, Paul Revere Williams knew this confrontation only too well. And in forcing him to learn to draw upside down so he could illustrate ideas sitting opposite white clients uncomfortable sitting next to him, or to inspect sites with his hands clasped behind his back should colleagues refuse to shake it, it was a confrontation that manifested itself

RIGHT: Karen Hudson is photographed inside the lanai at her home in Los Angeles designed by and home to her late grandfather Paul Revere Williams.

BELOW: The dome of the iconic Theme building at Los Angeles International Airport.

not in the sudden shock of racial violence but in the grinding litany of absurd social perversities that he was forced to quietly endure for much of his career.

And yet Williams's story is characterized by triumph rather than oppression. He became the first African American member of the American Institute of Architects (AIA) in 1923, at the age of just twenty-nine, and thirty-four years later he became the first black member to be inducted into the AIA's prestigious College of Fellows. Over a trailblazing career that spanned well over half a century, Williams designed over 2,500 buildings, many of them in his native Los Angeles, a city whose distinctive, architecturally pluralistic character he helped to create. Many of these buildings were lavish homes for

the stars of Hollywood's Golden Age, and the list of screen icons by whom he was engaged for this purpose is extraordinary. Cary Grant, Frank Sinatra, Barbara Stanwyck, Lucille Ball and Bill Cosby were just some of his clients, and in contemporary Hollywood Denzel Washington, Andy Garcia and Ellen DeGeneres have all lived in homes designed by Williams.

Williams designed public buildings too, including a number of civic buildings and public housing projects in LA and beyond. In a demonstration of his generosity, he designed St. Jude's Children's Hospital in Memphis (1962) for free for friend and comedian Danny Thomas on the sole proviso that his contribution be kept secret. Williams also designed one of LA's most famous buildings, the iconic Theme Building for

Los Angeles International Airport (1961). With its stunningly futuristic pop-art rendition of a prowling, skeletal dome, the building has become an enduring symbol of the city and of global airport design. It also embodies the pioneering thrill and exhilaration of the Space Age that gripped America in the 1960s, sometimes referred to as Googie architecture.

Williams was born in humble surroundings and knew hardship and struggle from his youth. Both his parents died from tuberculosis when he was just four years old, after which he was raised by a family friend. It is perhaps because of the stable home he lacked as a child that he became obsessed with the idea of designing idealized homes for others. In 1921, despite discouragement from family and friends, he became the first certified black architect west of the Mississippi in order to do so.

Three years later, remarkably, Williams established his own office and would spend the next several decades designing some of the most lavish mansions in Hollywood and Beverly Hills. What is remarkable about his designs is their versatility: he could turn his hand to any number of styles, including English Tudor, French chateau, Spanish Villa, Regency, Colonial, Art Deco and much more. What unites these diverse works is Williams's innate understanding of the aspiration hardwired into the Californian psyche, which he cleverly commoditized into domestic escapism. Inevitably his buildings symbolized glamour too, and his use of the swirling staircase became a signature motif.

The irony was never lost on Williams that for most of his lifetime his colour prevented him from living in many of the neighbourhoods in which he designed his mansions. But he was never cowed by the prejudice he faced, and he used it to drive him on to greater things. His resilient approach to oppression, evidenced in this poignant quote, establishes him as one of the most inspirational figures in 20th-century architecture: 'If I allow the fact that I am a Negro to checkmate my will to do, now, I will inevitably form the habit of being defeated.'

LOUIS
KAHN

UNITED STATES
1901–1974

HIGHLIGHTS
Salk Institute, Phillips Exeter Academy Library, Yale University Art Gallery

PRINCIPAL STYLE
Modernism

ABOVE: Louis Kahn

MODERNISM AND MEDIEVALISM ARE HARDLY ARCHITECTURAL STYLES WHERE WE FIND MUCH IN COMMON, BUT IN LOUIS KAHN'S EXTRAORDINARY BODY OF WORK HE FUSED THEM TO CREATE A STRANGE, QUIXOTIC HYBRID THAT PRODUCED SOME OF THE MOST INFLUENTIAL AND ACCLAIMED BUILDINGS OF THE 20TH CENTURY.

By the time Kahn came to the fore in his fifties, the International Style was all the rage, a style in which Kahn himself initially worked. It was not, however, the glass skins and steel frames of the International Style that really interested Kahn but two much older and obscure architectural pedigrees.

Born in Estonia to a Jewish family so poverty-stricken they could not afford the pencils to indulge his talent for drawing, Kahn emigrated at the age of five to America, where he excelled in his architectural studies at the University of Pennsylvania. But he would return to tour his native Europe at two key points in his career that would have great influence on his later work. First, as a young man in 1928, he was hypnotized by the walled medieval strongholds of Scottish castles and French fortified cities like the extraordinary Carcassonne. Then, in 1950, he returned to tour Italy, Greece and Egypt and was

ABOVE: The symmetrical beauty of the Salk Institute in San Diego.

beguiled by the romance of antiquity, specifically as preserved in its ruined form.

Both trips helped Kahn establish his inimitable style which, from 1951 onwards, we begin to see emerging in his work. While the International Style sought to create lightness and transparency, Kahn craved the opposite and used gaping geometric incisions to make quizzical carvings into monumental, monolithic lumps of heavy, load-bearing masonry. Consequently, Kahn was happy to break with the pervading Modernist credo that form follows function and instead created mysterious forms with hulking outer shells that did not necessarily reveal any clues to what took place inside, structurally or otherwise.

There was always a strong spiritual dimension to Kahn's work, and he used precise geometry to arrange

ABOVE: The Bangladesh National Assembly building in Dhaka sits against a moat-like body of water.

RIGHT: The Phillips Exeter Academy Library is a red brick fortress typical of Kahn's unique style.

his campus buildings into meticulously composed architectural constellations that appeared to have an ancient, almost astronomical presence. With their raw brick or concrete surfaces, this is what Kahn liked to refer to as 'ruins in reverse'. So much so, legend has it, that when the Bangladesh War of Independence was raging in 1971, bombers spared his Bangladesh National Assembly, then under construction, after mistaking it for some ruined historic site from the ancient world.

Eventually completed in 1981, the Dhaka building offers one of the most powerful examples of Kahn's maverick style. Rising messianically from a moat-like lake and complete with fixed drawbridge entrances, it appears like a vast fortified medieval keep onto whose sepulchral walls an invisible cosmic deity appears to have maniacally carved an array of geometric hieroglyphics. Kahn's seminal Salk Institute (1959–65) on the sweltering San Diego coast is less eccentric but maintains the same forensic geometric monumentality and is charged with arguably an even greater sense of elemental transcendent power. With its pair of muscular concrete pavilions symmetrically sliced by an arid courtyard canyon inscribed with a narrow strip of water and raised upwards like an altar, the whole sculpted ensemble is reverentially proffered like a sunburnt sacrificial prostration to the ocean onto which it leads.

Kahn's life and architecture also exist as vindication of all the quirky oddities that normally recoil to the periphery of mainstream life. Kahn was a short man whose face was permanently scarred by a coal-fire accident he suffered when he was three, and in later life he became characterized by floppy bow-ties and ever more extravagant comb-overs to hide his advancing baldness. He had a complicated personal life: though outlived by his wife of forty-four years, he had three children from three different women; one of those children painted a poignant cinematic retrospective of his father in the acclaimed 2003 film *My Architect*. So while it was undeniably tragic that Kahn lay unidentified for two days after dying from a heart attack, debt-ridden, in a toilet in New York's Pennsylvania Station, it was perhaps an appropriately odd eulogy to a life unconventionally lived.

BELOW: A spiral staircase within Yale University Art Gallery.

PHILIP

JOHNSON

UNITED STATES

1906–2005

HIGHLIGHTS
550 Madison Avenue, Crystal Cathedral, Gate of Europe Towers

PRINCIPAL STYLE
Modernism / Postmodernism

ABOVE: Philip Johnson

PERHAPS UNDERSTANDABLY FOR AN ARCHITECT WHO LIVED TO BE ALMOST A HUNDRED AND HAD AN EXTRAORDINARY CAREER SPANNING NINE DECADES AND SEVERAL ARCHITECTURAL STYLES, PHILIP JOHNSON WAS THE ULTIMATE ARCHITECTURAL CHAMELEON.

The first part of his career saw him as a committed champion of Modernism and in this vein he composed a number of purist Modernist commissions, most notably his own Glass House home of 1949 and, as an associate architect collaborating with his great competitor and early inspiration Ludwig Mies van der Rohe, the seminal Seagram Building of 1958.

Throughout the 1960s and 1970s, Johnson dutifully maintained the Modernist idiom, producing the obligatory glass skyscrapers of IDS Center Minneapolis (1973) and Pennzoil Place in Houston (1976), as well as the concrete podium structures of Washington's St. Anselm's Abbey Monastery (1960) and the Kunsthalle Bielefeld art museum in Germany (1968). But Johnson always had a wily and perceptive cultural ear, and – unlike many of his more dogmatic Modernist contemporaries – by the 1970s he had already sensed that Modernism had become too corroded by public disillusionment and failed social authoritarianism and that its game was finally up.

So he changed tack and joined the ranks of Modernism's ascendant successor, Postmodernism.

TOP: Thanksgiving Square Park in Dallas, with its spiral chapel.

NEAR RIGHT: Interior of the chapel showing its spiral stained glass windows

RIGHT: The Glass House in New Canaan, Connecticut

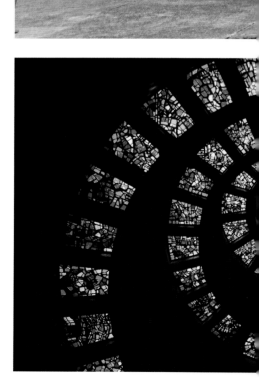

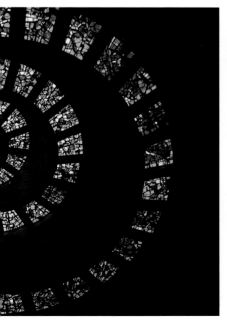

This is the style with which Johnson is most closely associated, and he became one of the movement's principal pioneers. His first work in the style gave clues to what was to come: the Chapel of Thanksgiving in his Dallas Thanksgiving Square (1977) is an abstract and whimsically esoteric whitewashed spiral that, though shorn entirely of decoration, is a subtly playful historic reference to the swirling pillars of Islamic minarets.

There had always been discreet clues to Johnson's historicist sympathies, even in his Modernist works, and there had been traces of loose classical orthodoxy in the plans and structures of some of his previous buildings. But while this was an affinity that Modernism could hardly tolerate, it was one in which Postmodernism revelled, with its trademark irreverent reinvention. Over the next two decades, Johnson, now in partnership with John Burgee, dominated the style internationally and used it to craft some of his most famous works. These include the sultry ellipse that is New York's Lipstick Building (1986), his salaciously gold and pinnacled Gothic skyscraper at PPG Place in Pittsburgh (1984) and his spectacular 3,000-capacity medievalesque mega-church, the Crystal Cathedral in California (1980–90), the largest glass building in the

world when opened and about which Johnson, with his customary dry sense of humour, slyly quipped, 'Don't build a glass house if you're worried about saving money on heating.'

But the worm turned again slightly when Johnson designed what is probably his most famous building, 550 Madison Avenue, formerly the AT&T building (1982). It is essentially a neoclassical temple, improbably recast as a 37-storey, 200 m (656 ft) stone skyscraper mounted above a stupendous eight-storey classical arch and topped by a gigantic broken pediment. Such blatant ornamentation and structural disingenuousness would have been anathema to Modernism, but it helped the building exert huge cultural influence. And while it was not the first Postmodern building, it legitimized the style among corporate clients and on the international stage. It also demonstrated Johnson's growing preoccupation with neoclassicism as well as neo-Gothic, the former again coming to the fore on his Roman-influenced Hines College of Architecture at the University of Houston (1985).

In the 1990s, when Postmodernism itself began to fall out of favour and Johnson was well into his

LEFT: 550 Madison Avenue in Manhattan, New York City.

NEAR LEFT: The Crsytal Cathedral in Orange County, California.

RIGHT: The Lipstick Building, New York City.

eighties, he metamorphosed again by experimenting with Deconstructionist theory. On the precarious, cross-braced incline of his Gate of Europe Towers in Madrid (1996), and even more so on the multicoloured, amorphous asymmetry of the Da Monsta gatehouse he designed for his 1949 Glass House (1995), we see Johnson heavily influenced by the likes of Frank Gehry and Daniel Libeskind and engaging in more daring, expressionist forms.

While some have criticized Johnson's various stylistic contortions as evidence of a lack of intellectual integrity, they misinterpret the fact that Johnson, like Frank Lloyd Wright, remained relevant and attained remarkable longevity by becoming a relentless American reinventor who, like Palladio, borrowed as much as he conceived. It is fitting that one of Johnson's favourite quotes came from his one-time hero Mies: 'I don't want to be original. I want to be good.'

OSCAR NIEMEYER

IT IS RARE FOR A SINGLE ARCHITECT TO BE GIVEN THE OPPORTUNITY TO PLAN AND DESIGN A CITY FROM SCRATCH.

BRAZIL 1907–2012

HIGHLIGHTS
National Congress of Brazil,
Niterói Contemporary Art
Museum, Cathedral of Brasília

PRINCIPAL STYLE
Modernism

ABOVE: Oscar Niemeyer

Wren failed in London. Haussmann, although an administrator rather than an architect, famously succeeded in Paris. Lutyens, Dudok and Le Corbusier succeeded too, in New Delhi, Hilversum and Chandigarh, respectively. But all these cities either existed before their trademark reinventions or had only sections rebuilt to a single architect's masterplan. Brasilia is that rare example of an entirely new planned capital city built to the all-encompassing design vision of just one architect.

That architect was Oscar Niemeyer, widely regarded as Latin America's greatest 20th-century architect. In Brasilia he crafted some of the most spectacularly monumental designs that Modern architecture

ABOVE: The Brazilian National Congress Building.

LEFT: The spectacular Cathedral of Brasilia at night.

has ever witnessed, sculpting a seminal series of whitewashed monolithic structures that spoke of the purity and dynamism of the Modernist ethos with a stirring organic fluidity and abstraction that has seldom been captured on such a scale since.

One of Niemeyer's principal tools in achieving this was his constant experimentation with the possibilities of reinforced concrete. He pushed the structural and engineering boundaries of what concrete could achieve to a level of futuristic, hyper-expressive, anthropomorphic sculpture that had a huge influence on later architects like Santiago Calatrava, Jean Nouvel and Amanda Levete. This influence was extended over an inordinately long career: Niemeyer designed his last building, the mirrored rotundas of the Museum of Popular Arts of Paraiba (2012), when he was well over a hundred; he lived to within a week of his 105th birthday.

Born in his native Rio to a middle-class family of Portuguese and German stock, Niemeyer had a carefree bohemian youth that took a more serious turn when he persuaded the great Brazilian Modernist architect and town planner Lúcio Costa to employ him after graduating in architecture from Rio's National School of Fine Arts in 1934. Two years later he persuaded Costa to invite Niemeyer's hero, Le Corbusier, to be a consultant on the commission for a new Ministry of Education and Health building that Costa had won. Finally completed in 1943, the 15-storey building, designed by a team eventually led by Niemeyer, became the world's first Modernist public-sector skyscraper and had a huge influence on the development of Modernism in Brazil and across Latin America. With its ground-floor pilotis and regimented concrete envelope, it also shows the extent to which Niemeyer's early work was influenced by Le Corbusier.

Niemeyer continued in a similar vein, and his career reached its pre-Brasilia pinnacle with another collaboration with Le Corbusier and others on the seminal United Nations HQ in New York (1952). Here, in the sweeping concrete curtain of its podium

RIGHT: The Oscar Niemeyer Museum, also popularly known as 'Niemeyer's Eye'.

BELOW: The Edificio Copan skyscraper in Sao Paulo.

building, we see the emergence of what was to become Niemeyer's trademark motif: the curve. Niemeyer spoke of being attracted to 'free-flowing, sensuous curves' which reminded him of the nature and topography of his homeland. He deployed them to soften and humanize his architecture and imbue it with an explicit organic resonance that further differentiated him from Le Corbusier. Curves appear constantly in most of the buildings he designed in his long career, including the Church of St. Francis of Assisi in south-eastern Brazil (1943), the Edifício Copan skyscraper in São Paulo (1960) and, perhaps most idiosyncratically, the naturalistically surreal raised eyelid of Curitiba's Oscar Niemeyer Museum (2002).

The curve is most memorably applied in the defining commission of Niemeyer's career, Brasilia. With his former boss Costa as chief urban planner, in just forty-one months from 1956 to 1960, Niemeyer built Brazil's new capital city as a galactic Modernist showcase for rational, futuristic urbanism. Of the civic, commercial and residential buildings he designed, the three most celebrated – the Presidential Palace, with its sinuous colonnade of billowing concrete sails; the blooming, ribbed hyperboloid of Brasilia Cathedral; and perhaps most prominently the sepulchral solemnity of the twin shafts and upturned saucer of the Brazilian National Congress – all perfectly depict the raw geometric power, naturalistic mimicry and awesome sculptural choreography which Niemeyer harnessed to craft his architecture and humanize Modernism.

EERO
SAARINEN

FINLAND / UNITED STATES

1910–1961

HIGHLIGHTS
TWA Hotel, Washington Dulles International Airport, St. Louis Gateway Arch

PRINCIPAL STYLE
Modernism

ABOVE: Eero Saarinen

ONE OF THE GREATEST AMERICAN ARCHITECTURAL FIGURES OF THE 20TH CENTURY, EERO SAARINEN WAS A MASTER OF DESIGN.

Saarinen collaborated with renowned furniture designer Charles Eames and the pioneering Knoll furniture company, founded by a family friend, to design a number of keynote furniture commissions, one of which, his curved and swivelled Tulip chair of 1956, deftly applied his Modernist precepts to a consumerist lifestyle and became a mid-20th-century design icon.

Architecturally, Saarinen is principally remembered for his sumptuously futuristic airports, which helped redefine aviation at a time when it was expanding exponentially into a mass consumer market. In his three showpiece terminal designs, Washington Dulles Airport, the former TWA Flight Centre

ABOVE: The TWA Hotel.

LEFT: Inside the TWA Hotel at John F. Kennedy Airport.

(now TWA Hotel) at New York's John F. Kennedy Airport and the East Terminal building of Ellinikon International Airport in Athens, he was responsible for embellishing the Golden Age of commercial aviation in the 1960s with the same romantic sense of glamour, anticipation, spectacle and escapism that the great train station termini of the 19th and early 20th centuries had created for the Golden Age of railways. Celebrated US Postmodernism architect Robert A. M. Stern has rightly identified the TWA terminal the 'Grand Central of the jet age'.

Along with Paul Revere Williams's Theme Building at LAX, Dulles and TWA remain arguably the most famous Modernist airport buildings in the world. Both opened in 1962, the year after Saarinen's premature death from a brain tumour but also the year that established him posthumously as one the most theatrically inventive Modernist architects of the day. While Dulles is clearly the more rational of the two, its swooping curved roof held aloft by a stunning inclined colonnade of colossal tapering piers provides one of the most hypnotically graceful architectural renditions of flight that Modern architecture has ever conceived. Inside, the melodramatic contrast between the solid concrete roof poured inwards like a sagging sheet and the soaring, light-filled ascendancy of the glass infills gliding upwards between the leaning piers makes for an operatic spatial spectacle of almost celestial beauty.

At TWA Saarinen again sought to capture the sequence of flight, this time in a far more organic and enigmatically zoomorphic way. Here a thin, sprawling concrete shell forms a curving roof and is supported by splayed wishbone piers, all of which suggest the wings of a crouching bird-like structure tensely poised to leap into flight. In a cavernous interior of curving balconies, arches and columns, Saarinen carved a spectacular, embryonic rendition of Space Age choreography so powerful that it quickly became as iconic a part of TWA branding as the aeroplanes themselves. The more angular Ellinikon (1967) lacks the scale and ambition of its American contemporaries, but even here the horizontal slice of cantilevered terminal held aloft over the airfield acts as a stirring geometric metaphor of skyward ambition.

Saarinen designed much beside airports and furniture, including Boston's Kresge Auditorium (1956) and Yale University's Ingalls Ice Rink (1958). Both display his trademark structural dynamism and experiment with the thin-shell concrete structures he would deploy to such electrifying effect at JFK. Less successful were his US Embassy designs for Oslo (1959) and London (1960), where he appeared restrained by historic context and compelled to produce stiffer, more constipated designs.

But this is perhaps unsurprising for an architect who spent his career preoccupied with the twin themes of flight and futurism. Outside his airports, these interests culminate most memorably on his Gateway Arch monument in St. Louis (1967), which at 192 m (630 ft) high is still the tallest arch in the world. With its leaping, parabolic form and glistening stainless-steel skin, it is almost impossible to believe that this abstract galactic portal was designed in 1947, when it seems salvaged from the sci-fi annals of future centuries. But it is an exultant testament to the extraordinary vision and ingenuity of Saarinen's architecture and its innate ability to poetically deploy flight as a conduit to the future.

BELOW: Main terminal of Washington Dulles airport.

RIGHT: Gateway arch in St Louis, Missouri.

MINORU YAMASAKI

IF ANY ARCHITECT'S WORKS COULD BE SAID TO FORM AN ALLEGORICAL TABLEAU OF THE LIFE AND DEATH OF MODERNISM, IT IS MINORU YAMASAKI'S.

UNITED STATES
1912–1986

HIGHLIGHTS
World Trade Center ('Twin Towers'), Northwestern National Life Building, Pruitt-Igoe Housing

PRINCIPAL STYLE
Modernism

ABOVE: Minoru Yamasaki

Yamasaki was the ultimate Miesian prodigy of the 'less is more' orthodoxy, and he applied it repeatedly to that most symbolic of Modern American art forms: the skyscraper. Yamasaki arguably understood skyscrapers more intuitively than any of his Modernist peers, and he was particularly adept at visually prioritizing their verticality. The iconic Twin Towers of his New York World Trade Center were briefly the tallest buildings in the world and, even before their cataclysmic destruction, one of the most

BELOW: Robertson Hall at Princeton University.

RIGHT: US Science Pavilion for Seattle's World Fair.

recognized architectural structures in human history.

And yet, like an architectural Icarus reaching too high into the sky, Yamasaki's work in its ideological extremity also holds the seeds of Modernism's eventual downfall. The fact that such an unusually high proportion of his buildings have already been destroyed by fire, terrorism or demolition lends a certain karmic validation to Modernism's demise. More significantly, it was their alleged inhuman scale, threatening the grain and intimacy of urban neighbourhoods, that substantiated accusations that Yamasaki was pivotal in Modernism's failure. And it was his work in public housing rather than skyscrapers that crystallized this critique. Historian Charles Jencks has described the 1972 demolition of Yamasaki's notorious Pruitt-Igoe housing projects in St. Louis as 'the day Modernism died'.

Born to Japanese immigrant parents in Seattle, Yamasaki first worked for Empire State Building designers Shreve, Lamb, and Harmon before establishing his own practice in 1949. In the 1950s and early 1960s his buildings initially became associated

with a US Modernist subclass known as New Formalism, which traded in the classical currency of symmetry and colonnades. It accounted for much of Yamasaki's early work, with the sleek classical temple of the Northwestern National Life Building in Minneapolis (1965) being one of the most prominent examples.

But it is for his skyscrapers that Yamasaki is mostly remembered, and during the 1960s and 1970s he designed dozens across America. In line with Miesian methodology, they are typically simple but powerful rectilinear shafts that through the use of expressed fins or striated columns exhibit overwhelming vertical emphasis that dramatically amplifies their height.

The strategy culminated dramatically in the foremost buildings of his career, the World Trade Center (1971). With its two 110-storey skyscrapers providing almost 15 million square feet of office space (roughly equivalent, until recently, to London's entire Canary Wharf financial district), never before

had tall buildings been conceived on this scale. Their verticality was also accentuated subliminally by the simple use of tightly packed structural columns on the towers' envelopes. The effect when looking up from its base was to witness hundreds of vertical lines hurtling upwards into an abstract celestial shaft that, on misty days, would pierce through the clouds into heavenly infinity.

To then double the effect by having two towers that perspective would compress into an immense mega-arch pointing skywards was an indication of the extent to which Yamasaki's work, like New York's early skyscrapers, was driven by Gothic allegory. It also marks the World Trade Center as the definitive example to date of the innate power of the skyscraper to excite the core human emotions of exhilaration and awe.

Even before they were felled by the worst terrorist attack in history, the towers attracted their fair share of criticism for their scale and articulation and seemed to endure in some minds as harbingers of imminent apocalyptic doom. However, a tragedy of sorts had already happened a thousand miles away in St. Louis: the monotonous hulk of Yamasaki's Military Personnel Records Center (1955) was almost destroyed by fire in 1973 and, one of his first projects, the controversial Pruitt-Igoe housing projects, had been demolished the year before.

Opening in 1956, Pruitt-Igloe was a vast public housing estate based on Corbusian principles and comprising almost 3,000 flats across 33 regimentally arranged 11-storey blocks. It was initially hailed as a stellar example of modern urban living for low-income residents, but by 1971 it had become so riven with crime, gangs, social delinquency and physical decrepitude that half of its blocks had been abandoned and fewer than 600 people lived in the rest. Debate still rages about whether the estate's demise was the result of design, mismanagement or society. But regardless, it does not do justice to Yamasaki's legacy that his two most famous projects live on in infamy alone.

LEFT: The gleaming iconic Twin Towers in New York City before they were felled in 2001's terrorist attack.

BELOW: The abandoned buildings of the Pruitt-Igoe housing projects in St. Louis.

I.M. PEI

CHINA / UNITED STATES 1917–2019

HIGHLIGHTS
Louvre Pyramid, John F. Kennedy Library, Bank of China Tower

PRINCIPAL STYLE
Modernism

ABOVE: I.M. Pei

IN THE 1980S, IEOH MING PEI DID SOMETHING EVEN THE GREAT BERNINI COULD NOT ACHIEVE 300 YEARS EARLIER: HE BECAME THE FIRST FOREIGN ARCHITECT TO EXTEND THE VALHALLA OF FRENCH CULTURE, THE LOUVRE MUSEUM IN PARIS.

In the 1670s, a furious Bernini had returned to Rome when his proposals for the Louvre's east wing were rejected, but by the 1980s, Richard Rogers and Renzo Piano's Pompidou Centre had already prised open the heavy international commissioning door through which Pei would eventually leap. In doing so, Pei created the defining building of his career and a piece of architecture that resonates poetically with the principles and approach of the greatest Chinese American architect of his age.

BELOW: The globally recognised glass pyramid of the Louvre Museum in Paris.

RIGHT: The John F. Kennedy Library, which Pei described as the most important commission of his life.

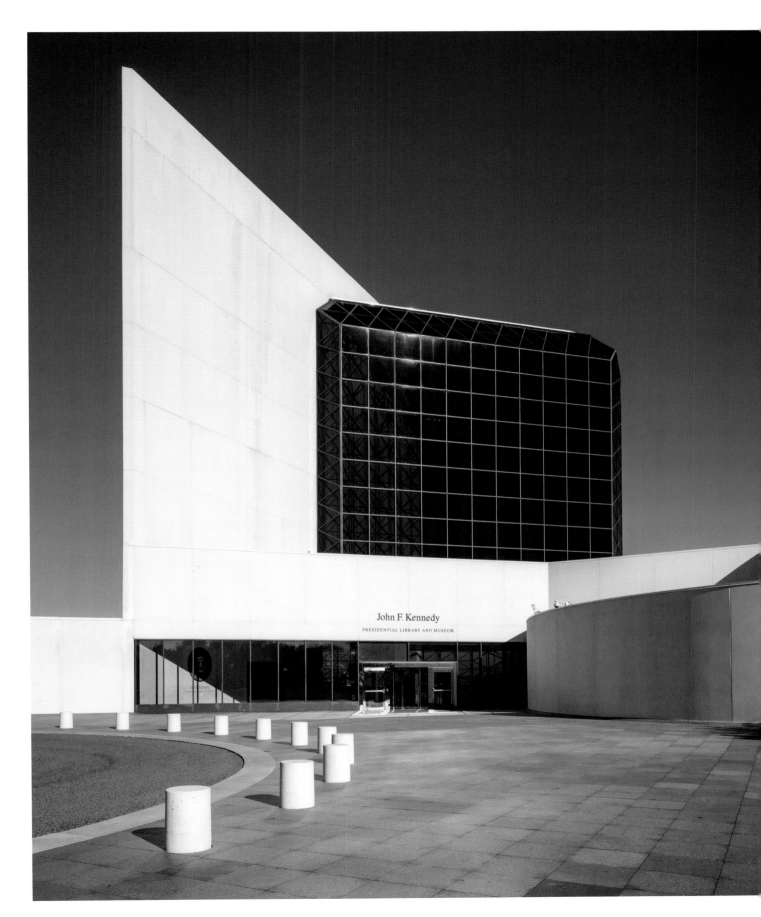

The Louvre Pyramid (1989) proved to be hugely controversial prior to its construction, inflaming the indignant ire of the French establishment and public, many of whom openly condemned it as an atrocity. Yet today it is one of the most recognizable architectural structures in Paris and is indistinguishable from the Renaissance surroundings of the grand courtyard in which it stands. The transformation is due to Pei's customary skill in reconciling his new structure with its enormously sensitive historic context.

Pei was an architect defined by his immense geometrical aptitude that frequently approached Cubist purity. He was renowned for being able to combine simple shapes (particularly triangles) with each other and with their context. With the Louvre he selected a simple pyramidal form that resonated with the faceting and inclines of the surrounding Mansard roofs. He ensured it was forensically aligned to the monumental urban axis laid out for the surrounding site by the great Baroque landscaper André Le Nôtre 300 years earlier, and he specified the clearest glazing possible so as not to inhibit transparency. The result

was a project that had the potential to end his career. Instead, it made it.

The contextual sensitivity, historic reconciliation and bold geometric competence that Pei exhibited at the Louvre Pyramid were characteristics that defined his astonishing seventy-nine-year career and were key to the considerable success that he enjoyed for much of it. When a traumatized Dallas sought to restore its reputation after the assassination of President Kennedy in 1963, its acting mayor turned to the practice that Pei ran in various guises for almost half a century, I. M. Pei & Associates, and asked them to design a new city hall.

Pei, also an accomplished urban planner, went out and wandered the streets endlessly, talking to residents about the city and analyzing its form and character. The result is a Dallas City Hall (1978) that deliberately rejected the high-rise format of the surrounding downtown in favour of a monumental yet unifying building whose steeply inclined envelope provided welcome shade from the blazing Texan sun and whose adjacent plaza sought to engage with the people whom the hall was built to serve. Its success also led Pei to five other projects in the city.

This approach typified Pei and, along with his near-constant smile and vivacious character, existed in stark contrast to the popular image of the Modernist Corbusian architect as a stern societal shaman unilaterally imposing his immutable will on the city. While he was never an outward Postmodernist, Pei tended to reject the stringent orthodoxy of Modernism in favour of a more intuitive approach grounded in responsive contextual analysis.

Over his long career, this methodology enabled Pei to maintain incredible aesthetic variety across his extensive collection of works. At his Mesa Laboratory (1967) in the foothills of the Rocky Mountains, rough-hewn periscopic towers appear carved out of the mountains themselves. At his acclaimed National Gallery East Building (1978) in Washington DC (one of several cultural projects he designed), its stark, sculptural monumentality is lavishly encased in the same Tennessee marble as its neoclassical West Building neighbour. And at his Fragrant Hill Hotel in Beijing (1982), Pei was inspired by the traditional themes of the land of his birth and created a sheltered enclave that was a cultivated (if politically contentious) response to surrounding nature and landscape. For Pei, no matter what the project, there were only ever two constants: context and geometry. In contrast perhaps to some of his Modernist forebears, both mattered more to him than style.

ABOVE: The impressive Bank of China tower.

JØRN
UTZON

PROFESSIONAL VINDICATION AND PERSONAL REDEMPTION ARE THE THEMES OF JØRN UTZON'S LIFE STORY.

Anyone who has ever endured a dispute with a work colleague, boss or client might at one point harbour a revenge fantasy where some great cosmic revelation proves that they and not their vanquished foes were right all along. Utzon's revelation did not emerge in time to prevent all mention of his name from being banned on the night Queen Elizabeth II opened his showpiece project in 1973, or even to earn him an invitation to the prestigious event. But with his Sydney Opera House – for which he endured torrential abuse, criticism and eventually exile during construction – eventually heralded as one of the greatest works of 20th-century architecture and one of the most famous and photographed buildings in the world, Utzon's reputation as a pre-eminent figure in Modern architecture has long outlived the animosity he suffered to earn it.

The problems with the opera house began as far back as 1957, when a thirty-nine-year-old Utzon, then an unknown Danish architect with a love of travel and a fascination for the works of Frank Lloyd Wright and Finnish Modernist Alvar Aalto, unexpectedly beat some of the world's foremost architects to win the competition to design a new national opera house for Australia. Judging panellist Eero Saarinen declared the proposals as 'genius', and Utzon relocated to Australia to build his winning entry.

It was not Utzon's youth or inexperience that condemned the project to perpetual acrimony but the state government's haste to start construction on what were little more than concept sketches. The decision led to an avalanche of structural problems, contractual disputes and design revisions

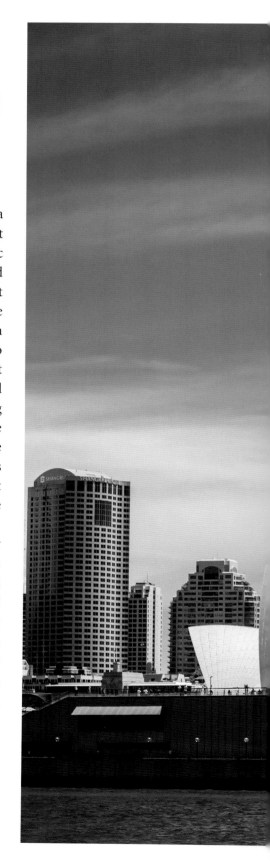

BELOW: One of the most famous buildings in the world, Sydney Opera House.

LEFT: Bagsvaerd church, copenhagen

LEFT BELOW: The National Assembly building in Kuwait.

RIGHT: A drawing of the North elevation of Sydney Opera House, including three photographs of segmented wooden models.

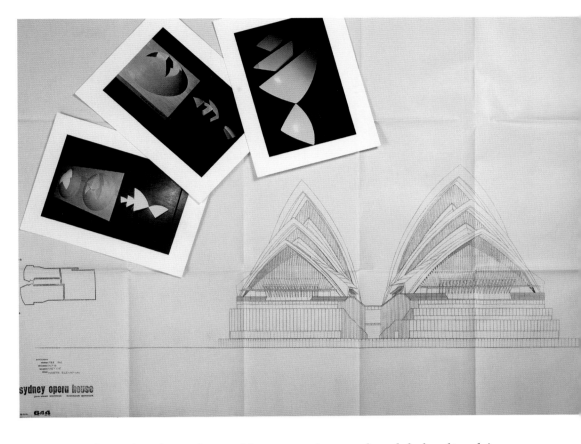

sydney opera house

that delayed the building's completion by a decade, amassed a colossal budget overrun of 1,357% and irretrievably poisoned Utzon's relationship with his employers. When a new state government refused to accept one of Utzon's periodic fee claims in 1966, he resigned with the building half-built and fled back to Denmark, never to return.

But time has proven that Utzon gave the world one its most exceptional pieces of architecture. The opera house's extraordinary design is based on fourteen crystalline ceramic shells of varying size rising from a waterborne podium like a herd of open-mouthed seals bobbing up from the water. The building combines the naturalism of Danish architecture with aesthetic and engineering sensibilities that were way ahead of their time. In fact, one reason for the project's tortuous gestation was the pronounced structural difficulties in achieving the complex spherical shells that the design envisaged. The acute limitations of the opera house's original acoustics, on which Utzon had no influence, were well publicized. But with its sculptural purity, visual dynamism and breathtaking originality, Utzon elevated Australia's presence on the world stage and created a global cultural icon. Despite his bruising Antipodean ordeal, Utzon resumed architecture practice impressively when he returned to Denmark. He designed a number of well-received and significantly more modest residential, retail and cultural projects, as well as the voluptuously enwombed interior at Copenhagen's Bagsværd Church (1976). His work remained marked by the quiet intimacy and naturalistic empathy that were his trademarks, and he also experimented with innovative prefabrication techniques by devising his modular Espansiva housing system.

His most significant work after Australia was the remarkable Kuwait National Assembly (1982) where, in its sweeping concrete canopy and monumental cylindrical colonnade, he not only channelled some of Saarinen's spirit at Washington's Dulles Airport but recaptured some of the organic energy of Sydney Opera House. But with Utzon joining Oscar Niemeyer as one of only two architects with a building accredited as a UNESCO World Heritage Site in their lifetimes, it is for his heroic Australian masterpiece that he will always be rightly remembered.

NORMA MERRICK
SKLAREK

ONE OF THE CYCLICAL CRUELTIES ABOUT
PREJUDICE IS THAT IN ITS DENIAL OF THE
ACHIEVEMENTS OF THE PERSECUTED
GROUPS, IT IS COMPLICIT IN ERODING THE
VERY IDENTITY FROM WHICH FURTHER
ADVANCEMENT COULD BE HARVESTED.

Invisibility rarely inspires, and few were more
constrained by this vicious circle than black
American female architect Norma Merrick Sklarek.

Over a remarkable forty-two-year career, Sklarek
worked extensively with Argentine American
architect César Pelli, was responsible for large-scale
commercial developments in California, co-designed
one of the world's largest US embassies, directed
the construction of Terminal One at Los Angeles
International Airport in time for the 1984 Olympic
Games and was instrumental in promoting the

RIGHT: The Pacific Design
Centre nestled in the
Hollywood hills.

BELOW: LAX Los Angeles
airport, California in 1984.

architectural development of that most American of consumerist symbols: the shopping mall. And yet because of her race and gender, she was formally recognized as a significant contributor to just one of these ventures, the US Embassy in Tokyo.

But Sklarek's life was still one of incredible achievement and eventual recognition. In 1954 she was only the third black woman to be licensed as an architect in the US, in 1980 she became the first black woman to be elected to the prestigious American Institute of Architecture College of Fellows and in 1985 she co-founded the largest woman-owned architectural practice in the US at the time, Siegel Sklarek Diamond. In a profession dominated by

white men, and during a segregated civil-rights era when she must have endured unimaginable prejudice and discrimination on the twin fronts of her race and gender, Sklarek thrived on adversity.

Born to Barbadian parents in Harlem, Sklarek won her architecture degree from Colombia University in 1950. Despite nineteen job applications to architecture practices, she failed to find employment and decided to join the engineering department in the New York Department of Public Works. Four years later she was employed by SOM, where she remained until she moved to the West Coast in 1960.

For the next 20 years, Sklarek worked for the famous Gruen and Associates firm in Los Angeles, rising to

the positon of production director and working for a year there with Frank Gehry. With Austrian-born Victor Gruen she was instrumental in developing the shopping mall prototype that was eventually exported to virtually every town in America and arguably did as much to shape the modern American suburban experience as the Ford Motor Company. During this period she also collaborated with another Gruen employee, César Pelli, on commercial and diplomatic projects, foremost among which was the US Embassy in Tokyo (1976).

In 1980 Sklarek joined Welton Becket Associates as vice president, and it was here that she oversaw the construction of Terminal One at and LAX Airport (1984). She finally set up her own practice with fellow LA architects Katherine Diamond and Margot Siegel in 1985, leaving only four years later in a bid to reacquaint herself with the larger, more complex projects with which she was most familiar. This she did when helping to design the Mall of America in Minnesota (1992) at Jerde Partnership which, with a

THE AMERICAN INSTITUTE OF ARCHITECTS

IS PRIVILEGED TO CONFER THE

WHITNEY M. YOUNG JR. AWARD

ON

NORMA MERRICK SKLAREK, FAIA

A PROFESSIONAL LIFE FILLED WITH CAREER FIRSTS,
SHE SHATTERED RACIAL AND GENDER BARRIERS
AS AN ACCOMPLISHED AND GENEROUS PROFESSIONAL WHOSE
QUIET DETERMINATION IN THE FACE OF ADVERSITY MADE IT POSSIBLE
FOR THOSE WITH DREAMS AND ASPIRATIONS WHO FOLLOWED.
THROUGH A SERIES OF PIONEERING EFFORTS SHE ADVANCED
NOT ONLY HER CAUSE, BUT THE CAUSE FOR MINORITY INVOLVEMENT
IN MAINSTREAM MATTERS OF THE PROFESSION AND THE AIA.
A POSITIVE FORCE OF CHANGE, SHE IS TRULY
THE "ROSA PARKS OF ARCHITECTURE."

MAY 17, 2008

MARSHALL E. PURNELL, FAIA
PRESIDENT

DAVID R. PROFFITT, AIA
SECRETARY

LEFT: The front entrance to the Mall of America in Bloomington, Minnesota.

BELOW: The United States Embassy in Tokyo and the Whitney M Young Jr award presented to Norma Merrick Sklarek by the American Institute of Architects.

stupendous floor area of almost 5 million square feet, is the largest mall in America. Sklarek finally retired shortly after its successful opening in 1992.

Sklarek was not the first black woman to be licensed as an architect in the US. No movement was named after her, and no building bears her sole authorship. But too much of great architecture is tainted by ego and too little credit is given to collaboration, and in this core human virtue – along with her superb technical expertise – Sklarek was virtually unsurpassable. Moreover, no individual is ever solely responsible for a building, whether they work alone or have their name emblazoned above the door of a large corporate practice.

What matters is that in Sklarek's tenacity, perseverance, professionalism and mere visibility in the face of stinging discrimination, and in her fostering the conditions that have helped empower women architects and increase the number of licensed black architects in America – from the handful there were at the start of her career to almost 10,000 today – Sklarek fully deserves her colloquial moniker of the 'Rosa Parks of architecture'.

FRANK
GEHRY

CANADA / UNITED STATES

B. 1929

HIGHLIGHTS
Guggenheim Bilbao, Seattle Museum of Pop Culture, Walt Disney Concert Hall

PRINCIPAL STYLE
Deconstructivism

ABOVE: Frank Gehry

HOUSEHOLD NAME FRANK GEHRY IS AS MUCH IMPRESARIO AS ARCHITECT.

Despite or perhaps because of the fact that he is one of the most famous architects in the world today and one of only a handful who is a household name, Gehry understands, as so many architects do not, that an essential role of architecture is to entertain. He does this in a number of ways. He has poked fun at himself in cartoon voiceovers. He is obsessed with fish and has designed various household items in their honour. He has a keen eye for consumerism and has created lines in jewellery, furniture and Vodka bottles. He often gleefully plays the role of cantankerous creator and has issued periodic public profanities in the direction of recalcitrant journalists and the questionable quality of '98%' of the world's architecture. But first and foremost Gehry entertains us with his buildings.

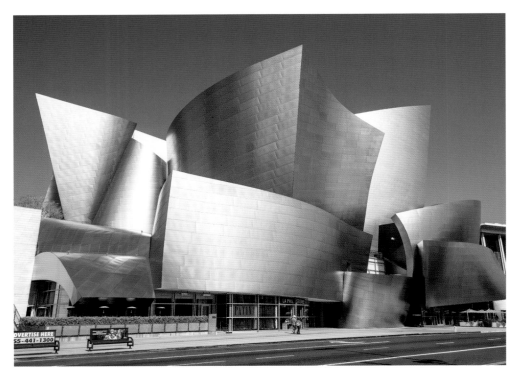

ABOVE: The Guggenheim Museum in Bilbao, Spain.

LEFT: The Walt Disney Concert Hall in Los Angeles.

NEAR LEFT: The Museum of Pop Culture in Seattle, Washington.

Gehry's work famously defies stylistic classification. Highly experimental and esoteric, his buildings are notorious for their amorphous forms, illusory aesthetics, high sculptural expressionism, billowing curvaceous profiles, sheet-metal cladding, occasional riotous bursts of colour and a total rejection of orthogonal geometry. Aesthetically, his buildings also appear caught in various stages of physical disintegration, with his extraordinary Lou Ruvo Center for Brain Health in Las Vegas (2010) seeking to mimic the neurological disorders it treats by seeming to crumble, cartoon-like, into the ground. If there is any movement to which Gehry can be considered to adhere even loosely, his crumpled and colliding states and the volumetric violence they engender align him most closely with Deconstructivism, the last defiant stand of Postmodernism that rejected traditionalism and

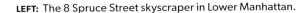

revelled chaotically in dislocation, disorder and disruption. The predilection for extreme visual and structural disorientation evident in all Gehry's buildings, and the ease with which this shock-value style lends itself to the contentious celebrity label of 'starchitecture' (which he vehemently rejects), has led to accusations that Gehry is merely an architectural caricaturist trading in the hollow caprice of cosmetic gimmickry. Ironically, his critics offer one of his most loved buildings, Dancing House in Prague (1996) – completed in collaboration with Czech architect Vlado Miluni – as evidence of this intellectual frailty. How can a building that aims to be a literalistic interpretation of the twirling embrace of Fred Astaire and Ginger Rogers be anything other than kitsch exhibitionism? Equally, Gehry's defiant reversal of some of Modernism's core ideological tropes, such as geometric purity and 'form follows function', has also irked some; with Gehry, *everything* follows form.

But to dismiss him as a superficial showman would be wrong. Gehry is a fastidious fabricator. Ever since his childhood in Toronto, when he would make structures out of wood and scrap metal, he has loved models, and in professional practice he navigates the design process and communicates his ideas by sometimes building hundreds of physical models to explore infinite iterations of his chaotic forms. In a world of uber-sophisticated digitized design (which Gehry also deploys), his is a raw and honest process of low-tech three-dimensional improvisation that reconnects with architecture's instinctive role as an informed manipulator of space, form and volume.

Gehry is also a master of reinvention, and he delights in the antagonist disruption of taking familiar typologies and turning them on their head. Take the skyscraper. Before his 76-storey residential tower at 8 Spruce Street in New York (2011), Gehry had never designed one before. Yet here he overturns angular Manhattan convention by assembling a rectilinear tower with standard sequential New York set-backs

and then mischievously infects it with a hidden virus that squirms and writhes underneath its metallic skin and causes its surfaces to crinkle and bulge like the thrashing surges of a trapped vertical wave. It is an effervescently avant-garde and virtuoso subversion of the Manhattan high-rise vernacular and remains New York's finest 21st-century skyscraper to date.

Finally, in what is arguably Gehry's most celebrated work, the Bilbao Guggenheim Museum (1997), we see his distinctive architecture become a powerful branding tool for transformative urban regeneration. Almost $4bn has been added to the Basque economy since its opening, and such was the astonishing scale of its success that the so-called 'Bilbao effect' is now coveted by cities across the world wishing to create new cultural institutions to revitalize their fabric and economies. If Gehry is architecture's mad sculptor, there is not only method to his madness but a touch of genius.

DENISE SCOTT
BROWN

RESPONSIBLE FOR THE MOST STINGING AND INFLUENTIAL REBUKE TO MODERNISM EVER WRITTEN, DENISE SCOTT BROWN PIONEERED A CHANGE IN APPROACH.

UNITED STATES
B. 1931

HIGHLIGHTS
Sainsbury Wing National Gallery London, Seattle Art Museum, San Diego Museum of Contemporary Art

PRINCIPAL STYLE
Postmodernism

ABOVE: Denise Scott Brown

Within *Learning from Las Vegas*, the seminal book she wrote with her husband Robert Venturi and theorist Steven Izenour in 1972, Scott Brown theorizes that all architecture must fall into one of two categories, duck or decorated shed. A duck clearly identifies its function without having to resort to signage. For instance, a Gothic cathedral based on a Latin cross plan is clearly a duck. So is Bjarke Ingels's Lego House in Denmark (2017), a museum dedicated to the iconic toymaker which is designed to resemble an oversized stack of its trademark multicoloured bricks.

RIGHT: Exterior of Seattle Art Museum with Hammering Man art installation.

BELOW: Entrance to the same museum.

ABOVE: The main entrance to The Museum of Contemporary Art, at La Jolla, California.

RIGHT: Sainsbury Wing, National Gallery London.

Decorated sheds, on the other hand, convey no indication of their function other than through the use of signage or applied ornament totally impervious to what their actual function is. For instance, a glass skyscraper could be an office or a block of flats and is only discernible by the sign above the door. A classical temple could just as easily be a hotel as a hospital. In short, the duck is a symbol; the decorated shed applies symbols.

Scott Brown's conclusions had been drawn by meticulously studying the garish theme hotels and neon-encrusted Americana of Las Vegas – a city then already dismissed by Modernists as tasteless, kitsch-infested, dystopian pastiche – and celebrating the rich semiotic language by which its otherwise banal commercial boxes would playfully shroud themselves in overt ornamentation in order to convey their function. But her seemingly innocuous observations enraged the Modernist establishment by severing the hallowed connection between form and function and justifying the blasphemous use of decoration.

Yet Scott Brown's heretical polemic struck a popular chord with a world increasingly weary of the elitist Modernist hegemony and eager to re-engage with local vernaculars. It effectively laid down the theoretical foundations for a new style that was as comfortable with pseudo-historicism and applied decoration as Scott Brown was: Postmodernism. By hastening Modernism's downfall and helping establish its successor, Denise Scott Brown and her revolutionary book emerge as two of the most influential architectural protagonists of the late 20th century.

The architectural team that Scott Brown formed with her husband emerged as the international pioneers of the Postmodernism movement throughout the 1970s and 1980s. Their influence extended beyond architecture into academia: both wrote and taught extensively before and after meeting when they were professors at the University of Pennsylvania in 1960, a year after her former husband, architect Robert Scott Brown, had been killed in a car crash. Scott Brown and Venturi became close collaborators, and it was her interest in urban planning that prompted them to visit and study the new city of Las Vegas in 1966, a pivotal retreat that formed the basis of their groundbreaking book. They were married the following year and remained one of the most recognized and influential partnerships in architecture until Venturi's death in 2018.

The buildings they designed together were as effective as their books in their ideological promotion of Postmodernism. Cultural buildings emerged as their preferred sector, and in a number of commissions, including the Seattle Art Museum (1991), the Children's Museum of Houston (1992) and the Museum of Contemporary Art San Diego (1996), they gleefully indulge in the playfully irreverent historicism and lavishly applied decoration that were first codified in *Learning from Las Vegas* and became such a distinctive feature of the Postmodern movement.

Their most internationally significant building, the Sainsbury Wing extension to the National Gallery in London (1991), where Scott Brown had studied under leading British Modernist Frederick Gibberd in the 1960s, became a totemic battleground between the opposing Modern and Postmodern factions. The commission had been won in 1982 by an uncompromising High-Tech proposal by architects Ahrends, Burton and Koralek. But the scheme's historic insensitivity led to a titanic public outcry endorsed by the Prince of Wales, who famously savaged the ABK proposal as a 'monstrous carbuncle on the face of a much-loved and elegant friend'. Eventually Scott Brown and Venturi's more conciliatory plans were selected, realized as a defragmented quasi-historical interpretation of the gallery's principal neoclassical facade. In this instance, as for much of the 1980s and 1990s, Scott Brown's decorated sheds triumphed over her ducks.

RICHARD
ROGERS

ALONG WITH NORMAN
FOSTER, RICHARD ROGERS
IS THE FOREMOST BRITISH
ARCHITECT OF HIS
GENERATION AND HAS BEEN
A PIVOTAL INTERNATIONAL
FIGURE IN ARCHITECTURE
SINCE THE 1970S.

In Britain and France he is arguably responsible for creating the defining building of the decade for three consecutive decades: the Pompidou Centre in the 1970s, the Lloyd's Building in the 1980s and the Millennium Dome in the 1990s. And in High-Tech, the radical new functionalist, industrial architectural style he pioneered from the early 1970s, he helped give late Modernism a final, defiant resurgence against the advancing supremacy of Postmodernism.

Rogers is famous for crafting buildings with a high degree of structural expressionism, where service and engineering features which are normally concealed are defiantly exhibited both inside and out. Much of his work played a significant and highly provocative role in the battle of the styles that raged between Modernist and Postmodernist factions during the 1980s. Rogers's ideological conviction often came with intense controversy. Many of his buildings are both praised and criticized for their frequently uncompromising and unilateral approach to contextual integration and historic sensitivity, and he became something of a bogeyman figure for a conservation movement galvanized by Modernism's retreat. But his enormous impact on the late-20th-century architectural scene is undeniable, and in his best work we see a futuristic and almost symphonic

BELOW: The distinctive facade of the Pompidou Centre, Paris, at night.

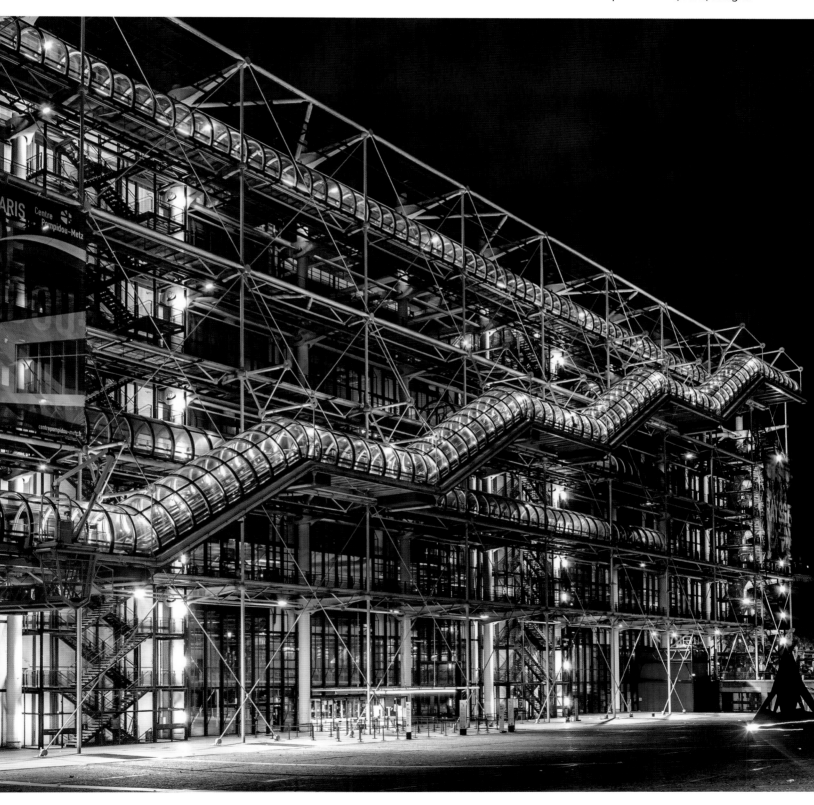

fusion between buoyant structural exposition and charismatic visual spectacle.

Born in Tuscany to an Anglo-Italian family, and dyslexic since childhood, Rogers schooled in England before winning an architecture scholarship to Yale. There he met fellow student Norman Foster, and a year after graduating in 1962 they returned to England and founded their Team 4 architecture practice with their future wives. While the firm disbanded just four years later, its early experimentation with metal prefabrication and structural display was evident in projects like Swindon's Reliance Controls factory (1967), widely considered to be the first industrial High-Tech building.

By the early 1970s, Rogers was in partnership with rising Italian architect Renzo Piano, and together they won the defining commission of their early careers, the Pompidou Centre in Paris (1977). With its extruded, cross-braced, Meccano-like exterior and with its services and circulation externally exposed in colour-coded tubes, it initially caused uproar in a city renowned for its acutely conservative conservationism, but it has since become one of the most popular museums in Paris.

Even more controversial was Rogers's next major project, now under the Richard Rogers Partnership: the Lloyd's Building in the City of London (1986). The building is essentially conceived as a large fortified

Academy, he presented a series of radical ideas for how central London's public realm could be improved. They were initially dismissed by authorities but later incorporated into old partner Norman Foster's 2003 pedestrianization of Trafalgar Square. Equally, in his landmark book Cities for a Small Planet (1997), he anticipated the current sociopolitical prioritization of sustainability and sought to influence a new generation of designers about the importance of responsible urban development. Between 1998 and 2009 he was also chief urban advisor to the British government and then to the mayor of London.

Perhaps as a result of this more socially conscious tone, Rogers's more recent work, now under the guise of the Rogers Stirk Harbour + Partners, has often struck a softer and less abrasive chord. The stunning Terminal 4 of the Madrid–Barajas Airport (2004) is arguably the highlight, a long, cathedral-like concourse centrally pierced by a stately row of piers over which a sumptuous, undulating timber ceiling unfurls like a sheet flapping in the wind. And even at the site of his fiercest battle, his Leadenhall Tower (2014) opposite the Lloyd's Building dispenses with the extroverted antagonism of its forebear and politely sheathes its superstructure behind shimmering veils of glass. Still High-Tech in spirit, if less so in execution; maturity has tamed the machine.

machine, with an armoured and windowless steel-plate exterior riveted by muscular sinews of exposed ductwork, beams and staircases and assembled with the aggressive, mechanistic functionality of an oil rig. At least Pompidou's footprint conformed to Paris's historic street layout – everything about Lloyd's was in open, pugilistic defiance of its historic context. Though undoubtedly a benchmark in the history of High-Tech, it vehemently divides opinion to this day.

Less contentious was Rogers's growing interest in urban renewal, an area where he exhibited acute social awareness and proved to be remarkably prophetic. In the 1986 London As It Could Be exhibition at the Royal

ABOVE: The Lloyd's building in the heart of London's financial district showed off the High-Tech ideal.

LEFT: The Millennium Dome in London's Greenwich Peninsula.

RIGHT: A detail from London As It Could be, showing two main axes: north-south from Piccadilly Circus to Waterloo Station and east-west from Parliament to Blackfriars Bridge.

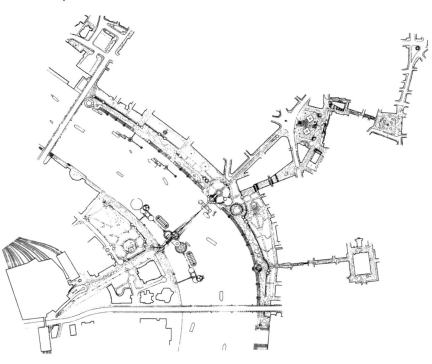

ÁLVARO
SIZA

PORTUGAL B. 1933

HIGHLIGHTS
Expo '98 Portugal Pavilion,
Iberê Camargo Foundation,
Museu Nadir Afonso

PRINCIPAL STYLE

Modernism

ABOVE: Álvaro Siza

SCORES OF ARCHITECTS STRIVE TO INFUSE THEIR ARCHITECTURE WITH A POETIC QUALITY, BUT FEW ACHIEVE IT WITH THE SCULPTURAL GRACE AND SURREALIST CADENCE OF ÁLVARO SIZA.

Born in a small coastal village just north of Porto, young Siza initially wanted to be an opera singer and then, more pertinently to his eventual style and career, a sculptor. But it was only after a trip to Barcelona at fourteen, where he recalls being 'mesmerized' by the work of Gaudí, that he committed to the profession in which he has worked from even before his graduation in 1955 from the University of Porto.

BELOW: Window in ceiling of Ibere Camargo Museum, Porto Alegre, Brazil.

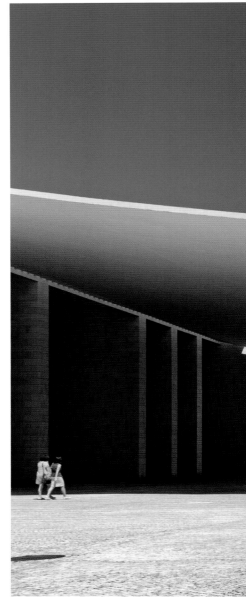

ABOVE: The canopy of the Expo '98 Portugall Pavilion in Parque das Nacoes.

Siza began to gain notoriety in the late 1960s, a time when Modernism was increasingly under attack. And yet, unlike some of his contemporaries, throughout his long career he has remained unapologetically committed to the Modernist doctrine and has created stark, severe and functional forms whose sharp geometries, spartan surfaces and deft manipulation of light and shade remain true to the strict minimalist precepts particularly evident in early Modernism. In this manner he has professed to being heavily influenced by the works of Alvar Aalto and the acclaimed Mexican Modernist Luis Barragán.

But Siza is more than just a thematic regurgitator, and his Santa Maria Church in Canaveses (1996) shows how. With its whitewashed cubical form, unadorned surfaces and primarily windowless expanse, the building initially appears to exert a sterile and subdued utilitarian austerity. This stands in polarized opposition to the tradition of polychromatic ebullience with which Portuguese ecclesiastical architecture is historically associated but is perfectly in keeping with chaste Modernist functionalism. The church's further incorporation of a mortuary and the inauspicious confinement of its bells to a pair of recessed rooftop shelves also serve

to heighten the air of stringent sepulchral repose. But then, like a sculptor cutting away at a piece of stone, Siza carves away from the rear of the church to form a cleanly scalloped apse. This then acts as a catalyst to introduce further subtle curves, and Siza gently bows and inclines one of the inner walls of the church, forcing its clerestory windows to emit a radial array of light and shadow that seeps celestially into the barren white nave. With these subtle deformations of surface, geometry and light, a functional interior erupts into a sensuous surrealist womb that mounts an endearingly poetic corruption of minimalist rationalism.

This theme of morphosis and the transmutation from one state to another is evident in much of Siza's work, and in its idiosyncratically choreographed nonconformity it summons the spirit of Gaudí. A more direct allusion to the great Catalan architect is made with the Bonjour Tristesse block of flats in Berlin (1984), where Siza's uncharacteristic use of sinuous curves and an organic profile recalls Barcelona's Casa Milà in leavened form.

A more typical sculptural assembly is found in his Building on the Water (2014), an office block for a chemical plant in Jiangsu Province, China, whose

ABOVE: Nadir Afonso Museum of Contemporary Art in Chaves, Portugal.

RIGHT: Church of Santa Maria in Canaveses, Portugal.

NEAR RIGHT: The promenade with "open rooms" at the Vitra Campus, Weil am Rhein, Germany.

swooping, elegant curves collide with razor-sharp angles to form a taut geometric knot. It is then dramatically and surreally twisted into place in the middle of an artificial lake. This theme of surrealism plays a recurring role in Siza's work, and in the Iberê Camargo Foundation in Porto Alegre, Brazil (2008), it memorably disrupts a curved white concrete facade by piercing it with the poking tendrils of enclosed angular walkways.

All these themes culminate spectacularly in what may be Siza's greatest work, his Portuguese National Pavilion for Expo '98 in Lisbon (1998). Here he sculpts two mighty concrete porticoes lavishly encased in ceramic tiles and positioned 70 m apart on either side of a large public plaza. Subdivided by a series of colossal sheer fins to form a Herculean asymmetrical screen of soaring portal bays, they firmly establish orthogonal regularity and exude tremendous monumental power.

Then, in a stunning shift, Siza drapes a vast, delicately thin 70m-long concrete canopy between

the two porticoes that bows towards the centre like a masonry hammock swung between two gargantuan posts. The effect is utterly extraordinary. Quite apart from the tectonic improbability of concrete assuming the tensile qualities of spun fabric, the simple contrast between the muscular porticoes and the delicately hanging awning creates a sculptural decadence wistfully dramatized by a haunting geometrical grace. Like much of Siza's work, it forms a poetic upgrade to established Modernist hardware by using sculpture and surrealism to rewrite the programme.

NORMAN
FOSTER

THERE ARE FEW ARCHITECTS IN THE WORLD TODAY AS FAMOUS AND COMMERCIALLY SUCCESSFUL AS NORMAN FOSTER.

UNITED KINGDOM B. 1935

HIGHLIGHTS
HSBC Main Building, Great Court British Museum, Apple Park

PRINCIPAL STYLE

Modernism

ABOVE: Norman Foster

With hundreds of buildings to his name in virtually every sector and corner of the globe, Norman Foster is now a pre-eminent architectural brand and offers a rare and elite architectural equivalent of the trademarked marketing heft of Apple or Coca-Cola. He is also unique in combining design ingenuity with commercial success, the holy grail that all architects aspire to but few achieve.

In a modern profession not necessarily renowned for business acumen, the irresistible question then becomes: How did Foster do it? Happily he helps us answer it by cryptically revealing his favourite piece of architecture: the Boeing 747 jumbo jet. Why? Because as well as Foster being a passionate flight enthusiast who drew planes before he drew buildings, the 747 powerfully encapsulates everything Foster's architecture is about. A symbiotic marriage of engineering and design, a jumbo jet is sleek, streamlined, efficient, industrial, compact, practical, prefabricated, compartmentalized and, in allowing for its engines to be easily replaced, superbly flexible. And that flexibility gives it a longevity which enables it to encapsulate the primal quality that motivates Foster and is tantalizingly embodied in his best work and is thereby central to his enduring popular appeal: the future.

Foster began his career in partnership with the other leading paragon of late British Modernism, Richard Rogers. The Team 4 practice they established was

ABOVE: The Great Court at the British Museum.

an early exponent of High-Tech, the late Modernist variant that prioritized structural expressionism and industrial assembly. After Team 4 disbanded in 1967 and Foster formed his Foster Associates practice (later one of the largest practices in the world as Foster + Partners), his early work kept firmly to the script.

But he added something else, a compacted clarity that was industrial without being oppressive and a structural approach that did not merely express the structure for the ideological sake of it but simplified and rationalized it too. This unique combination enabled Foster to inject the building typologies he

worked in with two key qualities that would also become defining features of his approach: innovation and reinvention.

This more streamlined, intelligent High-Tech enabled much of Foster's early work to be revolutionary. At the Sainsbury Centre for Visual Arts in Norwich (1978), he redefines the art gallery as a single, flexible enclosure. At the landmark HSBC Main Building (1985), as at Rogers's Lloyd's Building, the corporate rulebook was torn up to banish structure and services to the building edge in order to liberate the internal floorplate. And by relocating plant and services from the roof to a concourse undercroft to be distributed through the structural piers above, at London Stansted Airport (1991) Foster radically reinvents the airport as a naturally lit vault submerged beneath a lightweight skylight ceiling.

Foster, wisely, is no stylistic ideologue, and part of his extraordinary success has been his exceptional ability to apply this re-inventive clarity to all manner of historic building types well beyond the High-Tech idiom. So at the restoration of the Berlin Reichstag (1999), we see him resurrect its absent classical dome in a swirling spiral ramp ascending within a futuristic

ABOVE: The HSBC Main Building.

NEAR RIGHT: Apple Park corporate headquarters.

RIGHT: The Millau Viaduct, seen from beneath.

sphere of glass and mirrored steel. And at the British Museum Great Court (2000), he scoops out Europe's largest covered public square by reconfiguring former service yards as a magnificent neoclassical forecourt and enclosing it with a spectacular glass roof.

Foster's multiple high-rise commissions have also set benchmarks for innovation and adaptation, with his diagrid Hearst Tower in New York (2006) rising messianically from a retained 1920s base and his 30 St. Mary Axe Tower in London (2001) famously recasting the skyscraper as an elliptical nodule rather than a rectilinear slab. Ever the industrialist, Foster has also completed landmark infrastructure projects, including stunning new airports in Hong Kong (1998) and Beijing (2008), the sumptuously submerged tube station at London's Canary Wharf (1999), the sinuous blade of light that is London's Millennium Bridge (2000) and, most impressively, the sublime, ethereally hoisted 1.5-mile-long cable-stayed span of the Millau Viaduct in the south of France (2004). At 337 m (1105 ft) high, it is the tallest bridge in the world.

Boeing archivist Michael Lombardi has claimed that such was the 747's success in promoting commercial aviation that it was 'the plane that shrank the world'. By democratizing programmatic clarity and simplicity across all architectural styles, sectors and regions, Foster's astonishing career has done exactly the same thing.

JAN
GEHL

JAN GEHL'S PRIMARY OBSESSION IS NOT ARCHITECTURE BUT PEOPLE. EQUALLY, HIS OVERRIDING CONCERN IS NOT BUILDINGS BUT THE SPACES BETWEEN BUILDINGS.

Gehl has spent his entire career trying to reconcile these twin polarities, and in doing so has emerged as the most humanistic and empathetic leading architect of his generation. It has also associated him inherently with the theory and practice of public space. Gehl's work is consistently driven by his passionate belief that public spaces are the primary communal drivers for urban health, economic success and social well-being.

Accordingly, Gehl promotes walking and cycling as being infinitely preferable to car use, often lamenting with his charismatic wit that 'it's almost as if Henry

BELOW: New Road Brighton with its seating benches.

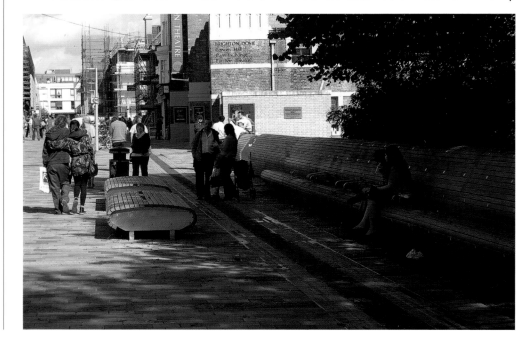

BELOW: Pedestrianised Strøget that promotes walking to the shops in Amagertorv, Copenhagen.

Ford is still alive!' and insisting that cities must be physically reconfigured to facilitate a more humane, people-focused redistribution of the public realm. His ideas have often been met with intense municipal resistance and, initially, intellectual disdain.

While many of these ideas are now intrinsically aligned with the sustainability movement that dominates current urban and environmental discourse, back in the 1960s, when he first prophetically articulated them, they placed him on a collision course with the prevailing Modernist orthodoxy. When Gehl graduated from Copenhagen's Royal Danish Academy of Fine Arts (KADK) in 1960, Modernism's hegemony was still intact, and patches of post-war cities across the world were being rebuilt with varying degrees of allegiance to the mechanistic ideological edicts of Le Corbusier.

But even then these were complete anathema to Gehl, who saw in Modernism's technocratic authoritarianism the totalitarian suppression of the human spirit as exemplified by the cultural supremacy of the motor car. Meeting his psychologist future wife shortly after graduation exacerbated this polemic, and he remarked that it is 'easier for architects to study form than life'. Acknowledging that Modernism did accommodate plaza-like public spaces, he dismissed these as often being 'no man's lands' that were too large and windswept to work.

Gehl's remedy was simple, and he still uses it today, in ever more sophisticated, data-centric ways. It involves exhaustively studying the prevailing social and physical conditions of any given site or city. This includes regular rigorous analyses of everything from climate, street furniture and age of users to desire lines, signage and behavioural habits. These measurements are then used as a basis for understanding context and framing an incremental design response that is sympathetic to it.

BELOW: The 16th street mall in downtown Denver with shops and cafes and green trees in the middle of the street.

RIGHT: Market Street in San Francisco, California with its cable car tracks.

The strategy sounds simple, because in many ways it is. But by adhering to it Gehl insists that urban and architectural intervention can attain a more intuitively human focus and thereby become more successful. For the first forty years of his career, Gehl, who became a professor of urban planning at KADK, disseminated his theories primarily through publishing and academia. Strøget, Copenhagen's main shopping street, was experimentally pedestrianized – with superb results – from the 1960s onwards according to his principles. During this period Gehl also wrote highly influential books that argued for the rejuvenation of public spaces and a more people-centric design approach to urbanism.

In 2000 he set up Gehl Architects in order to put his theories into action. This has now happened repeatedly across the world with remarkable success. The pedestrianization of Times Square and parts of Broadway in New York was based on studies that Gehl compiled in 2009. San Francisco's intermittently inhospitable Market Street is being tamed by strategies that Gehl has been devising since 2010.

Even the regeneration phenomenon known as the 'Melbourne miracle' – whereby Australia's second city has experienced remarkable levels of animated densification that have transformed it into one of the world's most liveable cities – has been largely attributed to the advisory planning role that Gehl has held there since the mid-1980s.

Gehl can be credited with raising the profile of public spaces to such a degree that even countries like England which have proved reluctant to practically implement his theories on a meaningful scale, have now effectively embedded the 'placemaking' principles he advocates into the cultural consciousness of the planning, design and development community. Gehl is an architect who may not be renowned for his buildings. But in reclaiming public space from traffic planners as an integral architectural concern, and in making our cities more human and liveable places, he has inherited the activist mantle of the great American urbanist Jane Jacobs and become the definitive urban guru of his age.

RENZO
PIANO

HIS EARLY CAREER MAY BE PRIMARILY ASSOCIATED WITH THE HIGH-TECH MOVEMENT, BUT PIANO'S APPROACH TO ARCHITECTURE CHARTS A MUCH OLDER PATH.

ITALY B. 1937

HIGHLIGHTS
Kansai International Airport,
The Shard, Whitney Museum of
American Art

PRINCIPAL STYLE
Modernism

ABOVE: Renzo Piano

Before the modern role of architect was invented, the architects of the medieval age were master masons, respected artisan craftspeople with an intimate knowledge of materials and manufacture. The concept of design, for them, was grounded in the process of construction. By creating architecture that stands primarily as an exercise in modern craftsmanship, Piano leapfrogs the centuries to identify with this lineage, one immeasurably enriched by the Renaissance masters of his native land.

RIGHT: The striking vertical expanse of the Shard, London.

BELOW: Whitney Museum of American Art in New York.

It is a lineage honoured in the name of his practice, Renzo Piano Building Workshop, and embedded in his own genealogy: he comes from a family of builders that stretches back generations. And with Piano's signature emphasis on the themes of transparency, engineering, modularity, light and a certain gentleness of touch, it is a lineage he has applied to materials across a wide range of styles, building types and scales. While this intellectual diversity makes Piano's own signature visual style harder to define, it endows him with one of the least aesthetically homogeneous portfolios of any leading architect today. Piano requires only two elements to always be in attendance in his work: craftsmanship and curiosity.

Born in Genoa not far from the stunning coastal hillside site on which he built his practice's main office in 1989, Piano graduated from Milan Polytechnic University in 1964. The following year he was employed by Louis Kahn's Philadelphia office, where he remained for the next five years. His first major building came after meeting Richard Rogers in 1970, when they formed a friendship that has lasted ever since. Two years later they won the project that propelled them to stardom, the Pompidou Centre in Paris (1977). While Piano is less keen than Rogers to define it as a High-Tech building, referring to it more wistfully as a 'joyful urban machine', it set the trajectory of his early career as one intrinsically concerned with structural expressiveness and programmatic innovation.

Both themes make recurring appearances throughout Piano's work but not necessarily within the confines of High-Tech, a movement to which Rogers was always more ideologically committed. After forming his own practice in 1981, Piano undertook a wide range of projects which show extraordinary versatility. The most nomadic of these are the laminated timber sails of the Jean-Marie Tjibaou Cultural Centre in New Caledonia (1998). The largest is the gigantic 1.7 km (just over a mile) elliptical chute of his 1994 Kansai International Airport (the longest airport terminal in the world), and the most civic is his Potsdamer Platz in Berlin (2000), where Piano assembles a series of buildings and public spaces that attempt to form a contemporary expression of the rich heritage and culture of the German capital.

Arguably the most successful period of Piano's career has been its latter stage, when his approach evolved away from structural emphasis and towards heightened transparency and precise detailing. In 2011 he dazzled Londoners with his first UK project, Central St. Giles, a riotously multicoloured office block adorned with articulated terracotta screens. Two years later came the controversial Shard in the same city, Western Europe's tallest skyscraper yet one that seeks conciliation through its tapering form and the haunting frailty of its fractured summit.

New York in 2015 saw the opening of the celebrated Whitney Museum of American Art, an art gallery innovatively reconfigured as a nine-storey industrial glass and copper stack punctuated by external terraces and walkways. That year also saw the completion of Malta's stunning Parliament House, an ornamental stone palace which relates exquisitely to local heritage and materiality and is as far away from High-Tech as it is possible to be – unlike the death-defying Paris Courthouse of 2017, a 30-storey tiered pedestal of successively smaller office blocks piled precariously on top of each other and encased in a shimmering translucent glass veil.

The genius of Piano's buildings is that no matter their scale, they can all be reduced to their details. Whether it is the thin decadent splash of the red roller blinds integrated into the Shard's glazed cladding units, or the rooftop sails of the Los Angeles County Museum of Art (2010), all Piano's buildings are a methodical assembly of minor crafted moments that give delicacy and refinement to the whole.

EVA JIŘIČNÁ

CZECH REPUBLIC B. 1939

HIGHLIGHTS
Prague Castle Orangery,
Canada Water Bus Station, Zlín
Congress Centre

PRINCIPAL STYLE
Modernism

ABOVE: Eva Jiřičná

RIGHT: The Prague Castle
Orangery.

THE CONSUMERIST COMMODITIZATION OF ARCHITECTURE AS AN ASPIRATIONAL DESIGN PRODUCT IS NOT A NEW THING.

Back in the 18th century, British neoclassicist Robert Adam and his brothers were highly successful in promoting an eponymous interior design style that could be purchased as a wide range of domestic fixtures such as fireplaces, curtains and lighting. Charles Rennie Mackintosh did the same, and his distinctive architectural style was just as commonly applied to furniture as it was to buildings. The trend accelerated

BELOW: Canada Water Bus Station in East London.

rapidly under Modernism, as its intrinsic ideological use of industrial manufacturing techniques presented a natural crossover from buildings to lifestyle brands; some of the 20th century's design classics came from the pen of architects Walter Gropius, Eero Saarinen and celebrated Danish design maestro Arne Jacobsen.

One of the greatest contemporary contributors to this rich heritage of architect-designers is the renowned Czech visionary Eva Jiřičná. Although she is a trained and practising architect, it is interior design for which Jiřičná is best known, and she has spent her distinguished career blurring the occasionally fractious boundaries between the two disciplines. Her buildings are often expressed as a sharp manufactured assembly of intricately detailed components, while her interior design commissions display deft spatial manipulation of light and materials. Perhaps most

associated with the retail sector, she has inserted highly engineered and conceptualized contemporary spaces into often historic buildings. But her signature product remains the staircase, which she has consistently reimagined as exquisite structural jewellery delicately expressed as cascading, crystalline sculptures of light, glass and steel.

Jiřičná was born in Zlín in the former Czechoslovakia and, in a decision reflected in the rigorous structural interrogation that would mark her future work, studied both architecture and engineering at the Prague Academy of Fine Arts. She graduated in 1962 before being attracted to the fabled zeitgeist of Swinging Sixties London and relocating there six years later. Initially working as an architect for the Greater London Council, she was eventually employed by private practices and spent

LEFT: Zlín Congress Centre in the Czech Republic.

ABOVE: One of Jiřičná's celebrated staircases in Somerset House.

the 1970s working on Brighton Marina and a failed plan for Westminster Pier. But a chance meeting with renowned fashion retailer Joseph Ettedgui in 1979, and the onset of the glitzy consumerism of the 1980s, catapulted her career into orbit.

Throughout the 1980s, Jiřičná made her name designing scores of elegant London boutiques for Ettedgui's high-end fashion chain Joseph, through which she finally set up her own practice. Her work established many of the interior design themes we now take for granted in luxury retail, including glass shelves, monochrome styling, minimalist detailing, high shopfront transparency and precision-engineered glass display cases – and of course a procession of sumptuous glass staircases, most memorably realized on her 1989 Sloane Street store. During the 1980s and 1990s, Jiřičná's work was very much the clinically

refined contemporary backdrop against which the glamour of London jet-set life unfolded.

Jiřičná's subsequent fame saw her complete larger non-retail commissions still charged with that same sense of meticulous detail and engineered glass. Her Orangery at Prague Castle (2001) precociously adds a High-Tech greenhouse to historic grounds, and her Canada Water Station in London transforms the prosaic municipality of a bus shelter into sinuous glass ribbon supported by an angular steel tunnel. Jiřičná returned to the Czech Republic in 1990, and her Zlín Congress Centre – an elliptical jewel box encrusted with a concertina of perforated metal casement panels and crowned by a spiky tiara of pitched trusses – is arguably her most poetic building to date.

But it is Jiřičná's epic staircases for which she will probably be most remembered. One of the foremost among these is her sensational Miles Stairs at London's Somerset House, a reptilian spine of glass-edged concrete that swirls and tumbles around a 20 m (65 ft) long perforated steel mesh column. Set in stark stylistic contrast to the neoclassical splendour of its surroundings, its sculptural decadence and dynamic engineering not only push structural boundaries but form another impassioned Jiřičná reaffirmation of architecture's critical role as the pre-eminent conceptual driver in interior design.

TADAO ANDO

ABSENCE MAY SEEM AN UNLIKELY CONCEPTUAL THEME ON WHICH TO MOUNT AN ENTIRE ARCHITECTURAL CAREER, BUT IT IS ONE THAT STELLAR JAPANESE ARCHITECT TADAO ANDO HAS HARNESSED TO POIGNANT AND POETIC EFFECT.

JAPAN B. 1941

HIGHLIGHTS
The Church of the Light, Hyogo Prefectural Museum of Art, Langen Foundation

PRINCIPAL STYLE
Modernism

ABOVE: Tadao Ando

This concept of absence may have been painfully familiar to him since childhood. Ando was born in Osaka 90 seconds after his twin brother, but within two years he was separated from him and sent to be raised by his grandmother, instilling a profound sense of loss that reverberated throughout his early life.

For Ando, absence also comes in the form of haiku, the ancient Japanese art of emptiness in whose desolate simplicity ultimate beauty is said to reside. The beguiling manner in which he has conveyed the theme of absence through his architecture over a fifty-year career has won him rock-star status from his legions of global fans (including the likes of fashion designers Karl Lagerfeld and Giorgio Armani) and has made him the most celebrated Japanese architect of his generation.

One of his most famous works, the Church of the Light in Osaka (1989), offers a captivating demonstration of his style. A tiny church covering only around 100 m², the building is a rectilinear solid concrete box whose windowless severity recalls the Row House in Sumiyoshi (1976) that helped kick-start Ando's career. A solitary puncture comes in the form of a splayed wall that slices into the

LEFT: The Church of Light where a cross is formed by the gaps in its structure.

RIGHT: Hyogo Prefectural Museum of Art in Kobe, Japan.

box (but significantly never touches it) and denotes the entrance. Inside the church's starkly unadorned concrete walls, an intimate scale and dim aspect exude a compressive claustrophobia that some have described as unsettling. But the church does have one mesmeric primary source of light, for behind the altar a thin, slender cross has been sliced into the concrete wall like tears in a veil. Through it, transcendent fissures of daylight bleed through the shadows and appear, when daylight conditions allow, like a burning monochrome crucifix piercing the darkness.

The effect is utterly sublime, and within this powerfully poetic arrangement lie all the themes that recur in Ando's work. His masterful manipulation of light. His forensic economy of detail. His use of simple, geometric purity. His affinity for thick, reinforced concrete walls and their raw, Brutalist expression. His reliance on the acute spatial contrasts between light and dark, solid and void and the allegiance to traditional Zen philosophies that this implies. And of course the profound, barren emptiness of the interior, this constant, haunting sense of absence.

Some of these themes clearly identify Ando with his Modernist forebears. The obscure, geometrically sculpted earthbound mass of his volumes recalls the work of Louis Kahn, while the dynamic use of concrete betrays pronounced Corbusian sympathies. It was in fact visiting Corbusier's buildings in his youth that inspired Ando to give up an itinerant career as a boxer and pursue architecture instead – a profession for which, incredibly, he never received formal training. Famously, Ando even named his dog after the Swiss master.

But Ando's work is intensely personal too. In practical terms his adoration of load-bearing concrete walls defies Corbusier's insistence that external walls should be structurally superfluous lightweight membranes. On a more conceptual level, the powerful spiritual resonance, poetic quality and naturalistic empathy that run through his work are unique Ando characteristics that barely feature in the approved Modernist doctrine.

Over an extraordinary portfolio of well over one hundred buildings, Ando has honed and fashioned his distinctive style. At the Hyogo Prefectural Museum of Art (2002), he juxtaposes angles and curves to create a dynamic structural composition which also features ethereal edge lighting as witnessed at the Church of the Light. At the Museum of Modern Art of Fort Worth in Texas (2002) and the Langen Foundation art gallery in Germany (2004), he dramatically sets his sculpted concrete boxes above water. And at the Lee Ufan Museum in Kagawa (2010), brooding dominoes of sepulchral concrete walls cut into the sky and chart the shadowy descent into the galleries.

The one enduring physical constant in all Ando's work is his beloved concrete. He has perfected the art of honing and shuttering it to the extent that it frequently appears as smooth as silk or, when its exposed formwork holes extend over curved walls, imbued with the studded buoyancy of leather. With his consummate ability to use concrete to regulate and refine the light, solidity and absence which are his trademark, Ando excels as the ultimate architectural alchemist, forever striving to conjure spatial form from emotional loss.

LEFT: Langen Foundation, art museum and foundation in Germany.

BELOW: Modern Art Museum of Fort Worth, Texas.

REM KOOLHAAS

NETHERLANDS

B. 1945

HIGHLIGHTS
Seattle Central Library, China Central Television HQ, De Rotterdam

PRINCIPAL STYLE
Modernism / Deconstructivism

ABOVE: Rem Koolhaas

THE MOST INFLUENTIAL PIECES OF WORK EVER PRODUCED BY RADICAL DUTCH ARCHITECT AND URBAN THEORIST REM KOOLHAAS ARE, ARGUABLY, NOT THINGS HE HAS BUILT BUT THINGS HE HAS WRITTEN.

Three years after forming his Office for Metropolitan Architecture (OMA) practice in 1978, former journalist and Architectural Association graduate Koolhaas published *Delirious New York: A Retroactive Manifesto for Manhattan* to tremendous critical acclaim.

Using New York as the definitive example, *Delirious* argued that cities are addictive, organic and cultural machines that act as metaphors for contemporary life and whose development is determined by the imposition of architectural programmes that 'edit' human activities. His follow-up book *S, M, L, XL*, was published seventeen years later and was a frenzied, 1,376-page extrapolation of OMA's (mostly unrealized) projects interspersed with new concepts such as the obsolescence of established architectural principles (i.e., scale and proportion) *if* architecture aspires to an existential magnitude that transcends physical dimensions.

Both books had enormous theoretical and graphical influence on a new generation of architects, with *S, M, L, XL*'s bold typesetting, vibrant colours and catalogue style revolutionizing architectural publishing and feted by architecture students of the 1990s. For the uncharitable, Koolhaas, like celebrated architect theorists Peter Eisenman and Bernard Tschumi, is part of a pretentious architectural intelligentsia that, after the 1970s rejection of their Modernist ideas in the real world, retreated to a philosophical sanctuary where those ideas could be exchanged without fear of realistic large-scale implementation and

NEAR RIGHT: The Dutch embassy on the River Spree in Berlin.

RIGHT: La Casa da Musica in Porto.

protected from undue public scrutiny by the semantic camouflage of unintelligible prose.

For his army of admirers across the world, however, Koolhaas is the foremost architectural thinker of his day, and his radical, avant-garde and urgent nonconformity extends into fashion, publishing, film and theatre and is pushing the boundaries of architectural possibilities into newer, more provocative realms. And in spite of the overt intellectualism that his critics might scorn, Koolhaas has decisively turned his theories into practice through a huge body of significant and unashamedly surrealist architectural works across the wold.

Perhaps the first major work on which Koolhaas's reputation for unconventional thematic disruption was established was his Dutch Embassy in Berlin (2004). Here a translucent rectilinear block is surreptitiously smeared with zigzagging diagonal recesses and projections that inch across its facade like monochrome graffiti. And at Seattle Central Library (2004), an awkwardly chamfered diagrid glass box gyrates upwards and outwards in an extreme attempt to let the form of the building follow its internal functions.

Some of Koolhaas's most dramatic works have been satirical reinventions of the skyscraper format, a process with its roots in the entrenched Manhattan

affinity that Koolhaas articulates in his books. At the 44-storey De Rotterdam mixed-used development (2013), three conjoined rectilinear glass towers are sliced at their centre and one in the middle, with the resulting eight volumes staggering and shuffling away and towards each other like a colossal game of Tetris. And at arguably his most celebrated project, the CCTV HQ in Berlin (2012), Koolhaas parodies the traditional phallic skyscraper by bending it and twisted it back towards the ground to form a gigantic asymmetrical feng shui loop that glowers apocalyptically over the city like the dislodged hindquarters of an invisible mutant presence.

With Koolhaas's reputation for structural dislocation and volumetric disorder, many have aligned his work with the Deconstructivist movement. But unlike Deconstructivism, which tends to reject theory, Koolhaas deifies it. Moreover, as his extensive Lille masterplan (1988) and other comprehensive

urban studies show, Koolhaas is an instinctive and impassioned urbanist who could never fully subscribe to the dystopian nihilism that Deconstructivism mischievously promotes.

In any case, in several of his projects Koolhaas has dispensed with his trademark zany choreography and surprisingly shown a nuanced restraint that approaches rationality and order. Perhaps because he is cognizant of traditional English suspicion of excessive intellectualism, his two London projects, New Court Rothschild Bank (2011) and Holland Green (2016), display a pallid, almost Protestant sense of purity, sobriety and calm. Equally, his cruciform Alexis de Tocqueville Library in Caen, northern France, and his Lab City 'superblock' outside Paris (both 2017) are almost utilitarian in their chaste angular moderation.

Rather than being a Deconstructivist, it is far more likely that Koolhaas defies classification and submits to no authority other than thought. It is perhaps this innate capacity to subject anything and everything to the conceptual minutiae of intellectual interrogation that summons Koolhaas's extraordinary command of the weird as well as the rational.

LEFT: China Central Television (CCTV) Headquarters in Beijing.

RIGHT: De Rotterdam mixed use development.

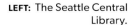

LEFT: The Seattle Central Library.

DANIEL LIBESKIND

LIBESKIND'S BUILDINGS OFFER THE MOST PROLIFIC MAINSTREAM EXAMPLES OF DECONSTRUCTIVIST ARCHITECTURE TODAY.

POLAND / UNITED STATES

B. 1946

HIGHLIGHTS
Jewish Museum Berlin, Royal Ontario Museum Extension, Imperial War Museum North

PRINCIPAL STYLE
Deconstructivism

ABOVE: Daniel Libeskind

With their jagged angles, severed forms, discordant geometries and eruptive violence, his buildings powerfully enforce the structural and aesthetic disruption, disorientation and dislocation that are at the heart of the Deconstructivist credo.

Libeskind's skill in achieving this so fluently has not come without criticism. Though it is a useful classification tool for the public, architects tend to abhor style, and Libeskind has been accused of shamelessly regurgitating this same angularly discordant formula in all his work. And yes, it is undeniable that projects like Manchester's Imperial

RIGHT: The Jewish Museum in Berlin dedicated to the memory of the Holocaust.

BELOW: The crystal-like extension at the Royal Ontario Museum.

War Museum North (2002) and his additions to Denver Art Museum (2006), Toronto's Royal Ontario Museum (2007) and Dresden's Military Museum (2010) all come with the same prickly, pointy, metallic fragmentation he has made his own.

And yet, despite this alleged stylistic monotony and Deconstructivism's visual celebration of chaos and violence, Libeskind's work is indelibly associated with memory, pathos and commemoration. His two defining commissions, the Jewish Museum in Berlin and his largely unrealized redevelopment master plan for New York's World Trade Centre (WTC) both serve to eloquently memorialize the most appalling human atrocities imaginable. In so doing, his architecture wriggles free from the antagonistic contrivances of Deconstructivism and attains an almost painful poignancy that identifies Libeskind as one of the most accomplished poetical agitators of his day.

Libeskind was born in Poland as the son of Holocaust survivors. The family moved to Israel in 1957 before emigrating to the US two years later. Shortly before gaining his architecture degree from New York's Cooper Union in 1970, Libeskind worked as an apprentice for both Richard Meier and Peter Eisenman. But he left both positions within hours, after falling victim to the parody of servitude that sees established architects initiating interns with assorted humiliations. In Meier's case it was slavishly copying his details, and in Eisenman's it was sweeping the floor. During this period Libeskind also married the woman who remains his lifelong business partner, and they honeymooned by touring Frank Lloyd Wright's buildings.

Libeskind then pursued a career in academia and, like the great Islamic architect Mimar Sinan, did not complete his first building until his early fifties.

The Felix Nussbaum Haus art gallery in Osnabrück, Germany (1998), was formed by a series of unsettlingly asymmetrical boxes complete with interlocking planes and sliced diagonal windows. Both building and programme (the gallery is also dedicated to fighting racism) were signs of the uncompromising architectural and social activism that was to come.

And come it did, hitting with searing commemorative force in what remains the defining built project of Libeskind's career. The Jewish Museum Berlin (2001) was the first and largest museum dedicated to the Holocaust of which, through his parents, Libeskind had suffered personal experience. With its angry zigzagging footprint scorched into the earth to mimic a shattered Star of David, and a hard, metallic envelope scarred and serrated by maniacal gashes that gape like open wounds, this is a visceral and intemperate composition that fully utilizes Deconstructivism's innate capacity for frenzy and rupture as a metaphor for a human narrative of senseless waste, desolation and loss.

And yet, in its graphic depictions of nothingness – as channelled through its empty Holocaust tower silo and a sublime sequence of 20m-high internal voids – and in its nihilistic representation of exile as a disorientating garden where trees grow from concrete trunks, Libeskind's work here attains a level of metaphorical fluency, poetic poignancy and raw emotional power that are almost unparalleled.

Now catapulted to international fame, Libeskind saw fit to repeat this commemorative prescription when he won the coveted 2003 international competition to redesign the World Trade Centre, which, with cruel irony, had been destroyed just two days after the Berlin Jewish Museum had opened on 9th September 2001, with its mandate of peace and reconciliation. Libeskind's Freedom Tower, a twisting glacial spire symbolically 1,776 m tall, captured the public imagination but not that of the WTC owner Larry Silverstein, who subsequently manoeuvred for Libeskind to be replaced by the safer corporate choice of SOM. The tower was completed as One World Trade Centre to a much-altered design.

But in the elements of Libeskind's master plan that remain, principally the two reflecting pools that mark the exact footprint of the destroyed Twin Towers and a plaza configured

as a sundial to be bathed in light at the exact moment each year that the towers were attacked, we once again find Libeskind's extraordinary ability to poetically elucidate memory through an architecture that invites reflection, reconciliation and redemption.

LEFT: Inside the Holocaust Tower at Jewish Museum, Berlin.

NEAR LEFT: The Imperial War Museum North in Manchester.

RIGHT: One of the two reflecting pools of the memorial at the World Trade Center.

ZAHA
HADID

THE LATE ZAHA HADID WAS, AND MOST LIKELY STILL IS, THE MOST FAMOUS AND SUCCESSFUL WOMAN ARCHITECT IN THE WORLD.

IRAQ / UNITED KINGDOM 1950–2016

HIGHLIGHTS
MAXXI, Heydar Aliyev Centre, London 2012 Aquatics Centre

PRINCIPAL STYLE
Modernism

ABOVE: Zaha Hadid

Along with Norman Foster and Frank Gehry, she was one of few architects who was a household name. Her untimely death from bronchitis at the height of her career merely served to crystallize her extraordinary achievements. She remains the first woman to win the world-renowned Pritzker Prize for architecture, she received two consecutive RIBA Stirling Prizes in the UK and she is one of only a handful of architects to have ever been made a dame. And all this for a Catholic-educated Arab-born Muslim woman from Baghdad who, in her religion,

ABOVE: Exterior view of MAXXI building in Rome.

LEFT: Heydar Aliyev Centre in Baku, Azerbaijan.

gender and ethnicity, neatly embodied an array of minorities not normally associated with international architectural success.

Hadid was as much branded image as gifted architect. With her famously flowing black robes, steely grimace and pronounced reputation for not suffering fools lightly, she carefully cultivated her public persona of authoritative virtuosa genius. Wisely she embellished it, to substantial commercial success, with a number of canny non-architectural crossover ventures in film, exhibitions, lighting, fashion and furniture which enhanced her public profile, particularly among a generation of adoring architecture students who worshipped her for her visionary encapsulation of the future.

It is in this very encapsulation, as conveyed through her spectacular collection of buildings and not in her image or marketability, that we find the true reason for her sensational success. From the jutting, Deconstructivist angles of one of her first buildings, Vitra Fire Station in Germany (1993), to the last completed project during her lifetime, the surrealist flying ship-in-a-bottle Port Authority Building in Antwerp (2016), Hadid pushed the structural, engineering, aesthetic and cultural boundaries of what was possible in architecture. Accordingly, her buildings have defined a new and uncompromising form of contemporary architecture that was wilfully conceptual, relentlessly dynamic and aggressively emotive.

Stylistically her buildings have clear Deconstructivist influences and trade in the rugged, aggressive juxtaposition of jutting, angular forms that the movement demands. But she imbues this with something unique and personal to her, a sense of flowing, swooping, ergonomic dynamism relayed through the dancing arcs of bulging curves and capturing a sense of restlessness, movement and urgency every bit as unpredictable as the frenzied imagined contrails of a fly zigzagging around a room.

Take her MAXXI museum in Rome (2010). Within an external concrete envelope of sharp edges and precipitous cantilevers, the interior appears as if conceived as an architectural race course and furiously pulsates with linear, monochrome tracks of walls, lighting, stairs and structure hurtling round hairpin bends, zooming over inclines and wriggling around corners. Whereas at her exceptional Heydar Aliyev Centre in Azerbaijan (2012), Hadid constructs a sublime depiction of fluidity by deploying a steel spaceframe and glass-reinforced concrete to carve an elegant whitewashed form of aching sculptural beauty. At its edges, the cladding elegantly folds and laps over its bulging frame like silky weaves of hair cascading from scalp to shoulders. Inside, the theme of synthesized fluidity continues, with a luscious, cinematically charged lunar soundscape of serrated ellipses and curving, celestial white spaces whose surfaces swirl and spin like whipped cream.

None of this was achieved without the use of advanced structural and design techniques, and Hadid's work is famous not just for its aesthetics but for the engineering ingenuity that turned her dynamic, gravity-defying concepts into reality. It was

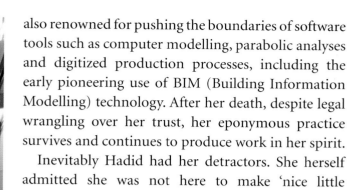

also renowned for pushing the boundaries of software tools such as computer modelling, parabolic analyses and digitized production processes, including the early pioneering use of BIM (Building Information Modelling) technology. After her death, despite legal wrangling over her trust, her eponymous practice survives and continues to produce work in her spirit.

Inevitably Hadid had her detractors. She herself admitted she was not here to make 'nice little buildings', and her architecture deliberately sought to provoke rather than pacify. Some chided her work for egotistical gimmickry, contextual insensitivity and a shallow objectification of architectural form. Equally, MAXXI was criticized for the cardinal curatorial self-indulgence of trying to vie with its artworks, and Azerbaijan's dictatorial tendencies made Heydar Aliyev a morally inappropriate commission for some. But a murdering Caravaggio tells us that rightly or wrongly history is careful to separate personality from performance. And by either measure, Hadid's trailblazing contribution to contemporary architecture is such that a future she did so much to envisage is likely to reward her with the perpetual greatness she deserves.

LEFT: Interior of the MAXXI Museum.

BELOW: The London Aquatics Centre, built for the 2012 Summer Olympics.

SANTIAGO
CALATRAVA

SPAIN B. 1951

HIGHLIGHTS
WTC Transportation Hub, Liège-Guillemins Station, Palace of the Arts Valencia

PRINCIPAL STYLE
Modernism

ABOVE: Santiago Calatrava

PERHAPS SURPRISINGLY FOR TWO PROFESSIONS THAT ARE SO CLOSELY INTERLINKED, HISTORY HAS GIVEN US VERY FEW ARCHITECT ENGINEERS. SANTIAGO CALATRAVA, ALONG WITH GUSTAVE EIFFEL, IS ONE OF THE GREATEST.

Calatrava adds another vocational quality to his works: art. Initially studying drawing and painting as an exchange student in Paris in 1968, he turned to architecture and then engineering only after stumbling across a book on Le Corbusier when returning home to Valencia after fleeing the student uprisings in Paris. Using this combination of artistic flair, engineering dexterity and architectural creativity, Calatrava has created some of the late 20th

RIGHT: Turning Torso Tower in Malmö.

BELOW: The Palace of Opera in Valencia.

and early 21st century's most striking and memorable works of architecture.

Calatrava considers himself primarily a sculptor, and his works are defined by twisting, curving forms that bristle with vivacious energy and expressive dynamism. Usually cast in resplendent white, his buildings' contorted geometries and gleaming skin can at their best provide a stunning ethereal transcendence that lifts the spirits and inspires awe. Calatrava's architecture is also conspicuously naturalistic and is rich in symbolic metaphor and zoomorphic and anthropological imagery. Straight lines and right angles are rare, columns curve and cluster together like ribs, and soaring vaults are shaped like the flying wings of a bird. The vigorous structural choreography required to deliver these forms has often led to comparisons with the work of Eero Saarinen, and Calatrava himself has professed his deep admiration for both Rodin and Frank Gehry. Like all three, Calatrava's work maintains a sinuous sculptural fluidity that becomes its principal visual trademark.

Calatrava's first projects were more structurally straightforward engineering and infrastructural compositions, but in them we see the first seeds of some of the soaring sculptural elegance that was to come. Zurich Stadelhofen railway station (1990) was the first of many train stations he has designed, but with its wishbone columns and tightly curving platforms it provides an early glimpse of his later style. In keeping with the engineering emphasis, this stage of Calatrava's career is defined by infrastructure as much as it is by buildings, and at the dramatically leaning arch of Barcelona's Bac de Roda Bridge (1987), the tensely extended catapult of Alamillo Bridge in Seville (1992) and the languid elegance of his Montjuïc Communications Tower in Barcelona (1992) we see the beginnings of his signature visual grace and advanced structural dexterity.

Over subsequent decades, this signature became more extravagantly applied on larger showcase projects. In the tree-like columns, vaulted intricacy and tall narrow arches of Toronto's Brookfield Place Atrium (1992) and Lisbon's spectacular Gare do Oriente (1998) we see Calatrava's work attain an organic, Gaudí-esque surrealism. And at the stunning Milwaukee Art Museum (2001) we witness Calatrava's first large-scale experimentation with the winged motif and movable architectural components. A vast rooftop veil with a wingspan of 66 m and a dramatic structure of swooping arcs and ribbed curves can be opened during the day and closed at night; it marks a masterly reconciliation of architecture, engineering and sculpture.

As does the futurist Turning Torso tower in Malmö, Sweden (2005), which, with 54 storeys and a height of 190 m was the world's first twisting skyscraper. The

building itself does not move, but with a pentagonal floorplate gradually rotating around a vertical concrete core and set within a stretching external steel frame, it twists a full 90 degrees from its ground to top floor and dramatically captures a sense of motion and elasticity rarely achieved by immobile buildings. Calatrava followed the tower with two of his most zoomorphic commissions, the ribbed reptilian exoskeleton of his Valencia Science Museum (2006) and the prowling mollusc shell of Valencia's Palace of the Arts (2006).

Two of Calatrava's greatest works are reserved for the railway stations on which he began his career. Liège-Guillemins Station in Belgium (2009) is a work of awesome operatic beauty. Comprising a spectacular 160 × 32 m steel arch and a monumental yet luminous glass and steel vault, it is arguably Europe's finest train station of the 21st century. And at the sumptuous World Trade Center Transportation Hub in New York, Calatrava's trademark naturalistic allegory culminates in his sublime architectural representation of a bird being released from a child's hand. With twin 45 m (150 ft) winged canopies thrusting skywards from a ribbed steel and glass cage that soars above a whitewashed concourse resplendently bathed in light, it provides his most poetic depiction yet of how architecture, engineering and sculpture can be inspirationally combined to elicit an emotional response.

KAZUYO
SEJIMA

JAPAN B. 1956

HIGHLIGHTS
Zollverein School of
Management and Design, New
Museum of Contemporary Art,
Rolex Learning Centre

PRINCIPAL STYLE
Modernism

ABOVE: Kazuyo Sejima

AS ONE HALF OF FETED DESIGN DUO SANAA, KAZUYO SEJIMA IS ONE OF THE WORLD'S MOST SUCCESSFUL AND INFLUENTIAL LEADING WOMEN ARCHITECTS.

With SANAA she is only the second woman to win the Pritzker architecture prize (after Zaha Hadid), and in 2010, the same year she was awarded the Pritzker, she became the first woman ever appointed to the role of director of architecture sector at the celebrated Venice Biennale.

ABOVE: Rolex Learning Centre
in Lausanne, Switzerland.

LEFT: Zollverein School of
Management and Design.

Sejima's work presents a clean, slick and glossy interpretation of Modernism, as relayed through the prism of contemporary design. It imagines a future of streamlined, clinical precision where a return to simple geometries and rational structure is enlivened by a new design culture of abstract forms and high conceptualism. For Sejima this future assumes the appearance of lavish, highly polished materials and reflective surfaces like mirrors, marble or stainless steel and is frequently delivered by a delicate, tectonic translucency that turns glass into shimmering, glowing veils of light. But despite this sophisticated, soft-industrialized approach, her architecture also strongly advocates a deep immersion in nature as subscribed by traditional Japanese design. Natural light is constantly prioritized, and sheaths of glass and sculpted views create an acute level of transitional fluidity between architecture and landscape, built form and natural form.

Sejima was born in Mito, the capital city of the Ibaraki province in central Japan. In a country that has a long tradition of female-only universities, Sejima graduated from Japan Women's University in 1979 and in 1981 was awarded a master's in architecture. She then worked for acclaimed Japanese conceptual architect Toyo Ito for six years, where she met student architect Ryue Nishizawa. She set up her own practice in 1987, where Nishizawa soon joined her, and in

1995 the two formed a new partnership and SANAA (Sejima and Nishizawa and Associates) was born.

One of Sejima's early works shows the high-concept direction in which she was heading. The Police Box outside Chofu station in Tokyo (1994) is an abstract and nomadic piece that sees a small police station inserted into a windowless black-painted concrete cube. A mirrored square and rectangle protrude through the cube, and it is punctured by a cylindrical (white-painted) aperture that extends right through the building. The project is small, but it perfectly captures the themes of reflectivity, contrast, simplicity and abstraction that have since become Sejima's signature.

Subsequent years have seen SANAA graduate to larger projects, such as the Kitagata Apartment Building in Gifu, central Japan (1998), where Sejima displays an eye for functionality as well as high-concept by humanizing and inhabiting external deck access around a large block of social housing. The first of multiple experiments with glazed translucent forms comes with the Glass Pavilion at the Toledo Museum of Arts (2006), where a swirling vortex of single-storey laminated glass walls curve and ripple as if caught in suspended animation.

A much more angular concoction is created at New York's New Museum of Contemporary Art (2007), where perforated steel veils applied to an asymmetrical stack of seven-storey glass and steel boxes enable them to glow like lanterns when diffuse light bleeds though the steel mesh. Equally, the Christian Dior Building in Omotesando, Japan (2003), is a sumptuous Miesian box that glimmers like a rectilinear lighthouse when milky or coloured light seeps through its draped floor-to-ceiling glass windows.

The Rolex Learning Centre in Lausanne, Switzerland (2010), represents a triumphant return to the voluptuous glass curvatures last seen at Toledo. A single-storey glass volume gently swells and falls to and from the ground like the random creases of a large sheet laid out not quite flat on a bed. Glass is also forced to accommodate a curvilinear nature that is expressed horizontally as well as vertically with a number of irregular, circular and oval-shaped courtyards cut into the floorplan.

In the shining metallic reflectivity of Tokyo's Sumida Hokusai Museum (2016), abstraction comes back with full force as a sharply angular windowless form is cut, sliced and splayed in a manner that appears to allude to cryptic, oversized architectural calligraphy. If Sejima's startling vision of the future ever comes to pass, then it will be a future where abstract concepts are brought to life and sheathed in a sleek, reflective chassis of metal and glass.

ABOVE: Museum of Contemporary Art, New York.

DAVID

ADJAYE

FOR OBVIOUS REASONS, ARCHITECTS ARE HABITUALLY DRAWN TO LIGHT. BUT WHAT OF THE DARK? CAN'T DARKNESS AND SHADOW BE AS COMPELLING A CONCEPTUAL DRIVER AND CREATE THEIR OWN ALTERNATIVE, OTHERWORLDLY SENSE OF DRAMA, TENSION AND SPACE?

UNITED KINGDOM B. 1966

HIGHLIGHTS
Whitechapel Idea Store, Dirty House, National Museum of African American History and Culture

PRINCIPAL STYLE
Modernism

ABOVE: David Adjaye

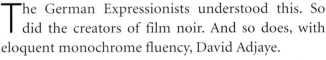

RIGHT: The National Museum of African American History and Culture, Washington DC.

The German Expressionists understood this. So did the creators of film noir. And so does, with eloquent monochrome fluency, David Adjaye.

Only a handful of living architects have been knighted, and David Adjaye is, at present, the youngest of them. In a profession where longevity is normally the key to success, the international acclaim he has received in his relative youth is extraordinary. A measure of this was his being awarded the most prestigious project of his career in the Smithsonian Institute's National Museum of African American History and Culture in Washington DC. The mixing of race and politics has an incendiary and painful pedigree in the United States, and when intertwined with the noxious invective of slavery it forms one of the most contentious and volatile areas in US public life. But although, or perhaps because, he hails from Britain and Tanzania rather than the US, Adjaye was able to create a building that has attracted almost universal praise and has managed to sensitively bridge the difficult gap between cultural celebration and honest and uneasy historical reflection.

Adjaye's architecture is indeed often characterized by dark forms and brooding tones. But he does not banish light; he merely channels it through heavy references to adjacent dark, sculpted forms. One of his early works provides a thrilling example. Dirty House (2012) is located in a heavily gentrified neighbourhood on the fringes of east and central London. It comprises a two-storey former piano warehouse which Adjaye

converted to an artist's studio with a flat above. The original building featured a simple brick, utilitarian exterior with punched windows. Adjaye replaced the lower tier of windows with mirrored panels brought flush to the brickwork, and the upper tier with clearer glazing to admit light inside. Significantly, the upper-storey windows maintain their deep recess, and the contrast with the flush lower openings are thereby indicative of the dynamic surface treatments Adjaye applies to much of his work, not least of which is his chequerboard, pockmarked Rivington Place (2009).

Most decadently, back at Dirty House, Adjaye lavishes jet-black anti-graffiti paint all over the exterior brickwork, turning an otherwise innocuous corner block into a fortified citadel that exudes mystery and intrigue. As the final flourish, he adds a heavily recessed additional storey on the roof which acts as the living quarters, with the lower black volume enclosing a single double-height studio. The attic is then overhung with a dramatically extending white parapet roof that acts as a luminous horizontal sail that exacerbates the weighty blackened presence

LEFT: Dirty House in Shoreditch, London.

RIGHT: From inside the National Museum of African American History and Culture.

BELOW: The Idea Store Library, Whitechapel, London.

below. This contrast is even more pronounced when the living quarters are illuminated at night.

The enigmatic touches displayed at Dirty House are signature traits in much of Adjaye's work. Rivington Place's rectilinear grey chequerboard is transformed into a black and white diagrid at Washington DC's Francis A. Gregory Neighborhood Library (2012), and the library is another typology he redefined in 2005 with his Whitechapel Ideas Store, which sought to reinvent the traditional library as a digital, communal learning resource for the 21st century. These are ideas that have since become very much mainstream. And as Dirty House suggests, Adjaye made his mark designing houses and has done so for other high-profile creatives, such as fashion designer Alexander McQueen and actor Ewan McGregor. Such is the esteem in which Adjaye is now held by the British architectural establishment that when one of these properties, Elektra House (2000), was threatened with

demolition due to planning contraventions, none less than Richard Rogers intervened to help save it.

But it is Adjaye's startling National Museum of African American History and Culture (2016) that remains the highlight of his career. The inverted step-pyramid structure is enclosed by a perforated bronze screen and conceived as a sculptural representation of a Yoruban crown, a sunburnt African-inspired presence amidst the whitewashed neoclassical monuments of Washington's Mall. Inside, a sequence of dramatic gallery spaces culminates in the Contemplative Court, where an illuminated fountain oculus rains down water from a dimly lit ceiling to invite solitude and reflection. Perhaps a museum dedicated to the best and worst of human nature is the most fitting commission for an architect whose work poetically navigates the shadowy hinterlands between light and dark.

PICTURE CREDITS

ALAMY

163, 168-9, 174-5, 176-9, 181, 182, 184, 188-9, 190-1, 194, 202-3, 206
16: Henry Yevele boss
17: Nave of Westminster
35: Palazzo del Capitaniato
36: Banqueting House, Whitehall
44: Louis le Vau
46: Plan of Palace of Versailles
49: Painted Hall, Royal Naval College
100: Portrait
102: Hilversum home
108: Villa Savoye
115: La Concha Motel
116: Portrait: New Yorker/Everett Collection
119: Staircase, Yale University Art Gallery
120: Portrait
122: Sony Tower
122: Crystal Cathedral
124: Portrait, Cathedral of Brasilia
128: TWA Terminal
133: US Science Pavilion
142: Bagsvaerd Church
144: LAX
145: Pacific Design Centre
146: Norma Merrick Sklarek Certificate
147: American Embassy, Tokyo: Rodrigo Reyes Marin/AFLO/Alamy Live News
154: Museum of Contemporary Art
158: O2 Arena
159: Lloyds Building
162: Nadir Afonso Museum of Contemporary Art
164: Portrait
170: 16th Street Mall
172: Portrait: Malcolm Park/Alamy Live News
172: Whitney Museum of American Art
184: Portrait: ULF MAUDER/dpa/Alamy Live News
196: Portrait
200: Zollverein School of Management and Design

ALL SOULS COLLEGE, UNIVERSITY OF OXFORD

52: Bust of Nicholas Hawksmoor

AUTHOR/IKE IJEH

6: Sydney Opera House
7: St Peter's Square

BRIDGEMAN IMAGES

11, 34, 38-9, 153
12: Portrait of Marcus Vitruvius: Stefano Bianchetti
16: The Jewel Tower: John Bethell
20: Basilica of San Lorenzo: Nicolò Orsi Battaglini
22: Santa Maria del Fiore dome drawing: Mondadori Portfolio/Electa/Sergio Anelli
26: Plan of Forbidden City: Peter Newark Pictures
27: Summer Palace Tower: United Archives/Carl Simon
31: Sehzade Mosque: Tarker
33: San Giorgio Maggiore: Sarah Quill

37: Queen's House, Greenwich: Stefano Baldini
41: St Peter's Square and Colonnades: Luisa Ricciarini
46: Collège des Quatre-Nations: Collection Artedia
48: Portrait of Christopher Wren: Heinrich Zinram Photography Archive
52: Staircase at Easton Neston: Country Life
55: Castle Howard Mausoleum: John Bethell
60: John Nash Wax medallion by J.A. Couriguer, c.1820: Granger
64: Portrait: Sir John Soane's Museum
67: Lothbury Court Engraving: Look and Learn / Peter Jackson Collection
68: Portrait: Heckscher Museum of Art / Gift of Mrs. Hubert de Jaeger
84: Portrait: Robert Phillips/Everett Collection
88: Portrait: Granger
88: Scotland Street School detail: Iain Graham
90: Glasgow School of Art: Mark Fiennes Archive
91: Detail Glasgow School of Art: Iain Graham
92: Portrait: The Stapleton Collection
95: Sketch No. 1 Cenotaph: Look and Learn / Elgar Collection
96: Portrait: SZ Photo / Scherl
98: Bauhaus School: Tallandier
99: Model of family house: SZ Photo / Scherl
104: Portrait: Everett Collection
105: German Pavilion: Hilary Morgan
106: Seagram Building: Collection Artedia
109: Gandhi Bhawan University: Leonard de Selva / F.L.C. / Adagp, Paris, 2021
110: Unité d'habitation: AWS IMAGES / F.L.C. / Adagp, Paris, 2021
111: Notre Dame du Haut: Jacqueline Salmon/ Artedia / Adagp, Paris 2021
128: Portrait: Tony Vaccaro
131: Gateway Arch: Granger
143: Sydney Opera House Drawing & Polariods: Christie's Images
148: Portrait
152: Seattle Art Museum Entrance: Omniphoto/UIG
155: Sainsbury Wing: Historic England
156: Portrait: Lionel Derimais/Opale
160: Ibere Camargo Museum: Dosfotos / Design Pics
180: Portrait: Stephane Couturier/Artedia
185: House of Music: Remy Castan/Artedia
190: Imperial War Museum: Stefano Baldini

CREATIVE COMMONS

14, 20, 24, 32, 36, 40, 56, 59, 94, 103
8: Statue of Hemiunu: Einsamer Schütze

GETTY IMAGES

44: Louvre Colonnade: Bruno de Hogues
65: Dulwich Picture Gallery: Oli Scarff
67: Sir John Soane Museum: Print Collector

70: Foreign Office: Heritage Images
71: Martyr's Memorial: Tracy Packer
72: Portrait: Chicago History Museum
76: Antoni Gaudi: Heritage Images
79: Casa Mila: Frédéric Soltan
79: Casa Batllo: Construction Photography / Avalon
80: Portrait: Bettmann
81: Wainwright Building: Raymond Boyd
82: Carson Pirie Scott Building: Bettmann
87: Johnson Wax Headquarters: Buyenlarge
97: Walter Gropius House: Paul Marotta
107: Lafayette Park: Chicago History Museum
108: Portrait
112: Portrait: Los Angeles Times
113: Karen Hudson: Mel Melcon/Los Angeles Times
132: Portrait: Bettmann
135: Pruitt-Igoe Housing Projects: Bettmann
136: Portrait: Jack Mitchell
140: Portrait: Bettmann
152: Portrait: Gary Gershoff
160: Portrait: Gonzalo Marroquin
168: Portrait: The Sydney Morning Herald
171: San Francisco streets: Justin Sullivan
192: Portrait: Franco Origlia
200: Portrait: Vincenzo Pinto / AFP
204: Portrait: Tristan Fewings
207: Interior Nationa Museum of African American History and Culture: Walter McBride

MARY EVANS PICTURE LIBRARY

56: Plan of Castle Howard

ROGERS STIRK HARBOUR + PARTNERS

159: Detail from *London As It Could Be*

SHUTTERSTOCK

9, 10, 11, 13, 15, 21, 23, 25, 27, 30, 41, 43, 47, 50, 53, 78, 85, 93, 118 (2), 121, 125, 126, 138, 139, 141, 142, 148, 161, 167, 173, 186, 192-3, 196, 197, 198-9
51: Hampton Court Palace: Malcolm P. Chapman
18: Canterbury Cathedral Cloister Garden: Roman Babakin
19: Canterbury Cathedral: A.G. Baxter
28-29: Bust of Mimar Sinan and Selimiye Mosque: Ihsan Gercelman
42: Fountain of the Four Rivers: Federico Curcio
48: St Paul's Cathedral: Songquan Deng
54: St Mary Woolnoth Church: Roman Babkin
57: Castle Howard: Leonid Andronov
58: Blenheim Palace: Simon Edge
60: Buckingham Palace: HVRIS
61: Regent Street: Ron Ellis
62: Carlton House Terrace: Paula French
63: Royal Pavilion: Patchamol Jensatienwong
66: Bank of England: N. M. Bear

69: St Pancras Station: Madrugada Verde
71: Prince Albert Memorial: cowardlion
73: Flatiron building: Stuart Monk
74: Grand Union Station, Washington DC: Andrea Izzotti
75: Selfridges: Zotov Dmitrii
77: Sagrada Familia: Valery Egorov
83: Guaranty Building: Felix Lipov
83: Interior staircase, Guaranty Building: Heather Shimmin
84: Fallingwater: Larry Yung
86: Guggenheim Museum: Tinnaporn Sathapornnanont
89: Willow Tearooms: Claudio Divizia
95: Cenotaph: David Burrows
98: Fagus Factory: Igor Marx
100: Hilversum: Pieter Roovers
101: Hilversum: Nigel Wiggins
107: Interior German Pavilion: Joan Bautista
112: LAX: Carlos A Torres
114: Guardian Angel Church: Leonard Zhukovsky
117: Salk Institute: Andriy Blokhin
120: Chapel Stained Glass Window: James Kirkikis
121: The Glass House: Ritu Manoj Jethani
123: Lipstick Building: Artem Avetisyan
127: Oscar Niemeyer Museum: Gregorio Koji
129: TWA Hotel: Leonard Zhukovsky
130: Washington Dulles Airport: Joe Ravi
132: Robertson Hall: E Q Roy
134: World Trade Center: Joseph Sohm
136: Louvre Pyramid: Florin Cirstoc
137: John F. Kennedy Library: Marcio Jose Bastos Silva
146: Mall of America: Brett Welcher
148: Walt Disney Concert Hall: Sean Pavone
149: Guggenheim Museum, Bilbao: Iakov Filimonov
150: 8 Spruce Street: E Q Roy
151: Dancing House: Vladimir Sazonov
157: Pompidou Centre: Robert Napiorkowski
165: Great Court, British Museum: Alex Segre
166: HSBC Main Building: Christian Mueller
167: Apple Park Headquarters: Felix Mizioznikov
180: Church of Light: Avim Wu
183: Modern Art Museum, Texas: ShengYing Lin
187: De Rotterdam: Victor van Bochove
195: London Aquatic Centre: A C Manley
201: Rolex Learning Centre: Mihai-Bogdan Lazar
205: National Museum of African American History and Culture: Joseph Sohm

SMITHSONIAN INSTITUTE

144: Portrait

ACKNOWLEDGEMENTS

First and foremost I'd like to thank my commissioning editor Tania O'Donnell whose warm encouragement and infectious enthusiasm helped make this book a joy to write and research. I'd also like to thank Stan Carey whose superb editing was able to faithfully distill each architect's entry while still capturing the essence and impact of their work. I'd like to thank my family and particularly my wife and son for their patient support while I was completing this book in the surreal days before the 2020 lockdown. Thanks too to Paul Newman whose depiction of an embattled architect in the *Towering Inferno* (1974) helped convince me as a child that architects are human too. And I'd finally like to thank Christopher Wren and John Nash for helping build the London that made me fall in love with architecture.